Strategies for National Sustainable Development

A Handbook for their Planning and Implementation

Jeremy Carew-Reid • Robert Prescott-Allen
Stephen Bass • Barry Dalal-Clayton

IUCN
The World Conservation Union

IIED
INTERNATIONAL
INSTITUTE FOR
ENVIRONMENT AND
DEVELOPMENT

EARTHSCAN
Earthscan Publications Ltd, London

Strategies for National Sustainable Development: A Handbook for their Planning and Implementation was made possible by the generous support of: Canadian International Development Agency; International Development Research Centre Canada; Overseas Development Administration, UK; Royal Norwegian Ministry of Foreign Affairs; Swedish International Development Authority; United Nations Development Programme

Published by: Earthscan Publications, in association with IUCN and IIED (1994)

Citation: Carew-Reid, J, Prescott-Allen, R, Bass, S and Dalal-Clayton, DB (1994). Strategies for National Sustainable Development: A Handbook for their Planning and Implementation. IIED and IUCN.

ISBN: 1 85383 193 X

Illustrations by: Christine Bass

Design by: Patricia Halladay

Available from: Earthscan Publications, 120 Pentonville Road, London N1 9JN, UK
IUCN, Rue Mauverney 28, CH 1196 Gland, Switzerland; and
IIED, 3 Endsleigh Street, London, WC1H 0DD, UK

Printed and bound in the UK by Chromocraft Ltd., Feltham, England..

Printed on recycled paper.

The IUCN Strategies for Sustainable Development Handbook Series

This handbook is one in a series being produced by IUCN and its partners to assist countries and communities implement Agenda 21, the action programme of the United Nations Conference on Environment and Development. The series will include handbooks on national strategies for sustainable development, local strategies, assessing progress towards sustainability, biodiversity action plans, involving indigenous peoples, and on integrating population and resource use planning; and regular companion volumes of case studies addressing the key issues of concern to strategy implementation.

Many international agreements and action plans now call for countries to undertake national strategies. These strategies seek to involve communities in united approaches to sustainable development. Some are sectoral, such as tropical forest strategies, others are thematic, covering topics such as biodiversity, education or climate change. Still others, such as national conservation strategies and national environment action plans, are evolving to become more comprehensive processes, drawing together economic, social and environmental development actions. This handbook is for people involved in strategies. It draws on experiences in different regions of the world to present options and examples of the role of strategies in sustainable development.

IUCN: The World Conservation Union

Founded in 1948, The World Conservation Union brings together states, government agencies and a diverse range of non-governmental organizations in a unique world partnership — over 800 members in all — spread across some 125 countries.

As a union, IUCN seeks to influence, encourage and assist societies throughout the world to conserve the integrity and diversity of nature and to ensure that any use of natural resources is equitable and ecologically sustainable.

The World Conservation Union builds on the strength of its members, networks and partners to enhance their capacity and support global alliances to safeguard natural resources at local, regional and global levels.

IIED: International Institute for Environment and Development

IIED is an independent, non-profit organization that seeks to promote sustainable patterns of world development through research, services, training, policy studies, consensus-building and public information. Established in 1971, the Institute advises policy-makers and supports and collaborates with Southern specialists and institutions working with, or on behalf of, governments and international agencies, the academic community, foundations and non-governmental organizations, community organizations, and the people they represent.

Focusing on the links between economic development, the environment and human needs, the Institute has research programmes in a number of areas critical to sustainable development, including human settlements, sustainable agriculture, environmental planning and management, forestry, drylands, environmental economics and climate change.

IUCN
Rue Mauverney 28
CH-1196 Gland
Switzerland
Tel: (41) 22 999 0001
Fax: (41) 22 999 0002

IIED
3 Endsleigh Street
London, WC1H 0DD
United Kingdom
Tel: (44) 71 388 2117
Fax: (44) 71 388 2826

Contents

Foreword

At the United Nations Conference on Environment and Development (UNCED) held in Rio de Janeiro in June 1992, the governments of the world agreed to plan for a sustainable future. All countries committed themselves to undertaking sustainable development strategies involving the key sectors and actors. This was a significant breakthrough.

Of course, attempts at integrated planning and action across the economic, social and environmental spheres are not new. It has been tried before, albeit inadequately. IIED and IUCN were convinced that the world would benefit from drawing together the lessons of this experience.

This handbook has taken two years to put together. It combines 14 years of comprehensive strategy experience in every continent, gathered by many practitioners who have been involved in past strategies and green plans. It is itself a result of a participation process.

There is no doubt that this distillation of lessons learned is timely. Governments must act on Agenda 21 and many state members of IUCN are committed to implementing Caring for the Earth. Both global initiatives complement each other. Then there is the willingness of the World Bank to bring their National Environmental Action Plan process nearer to the wider vision of a national strategy. All in all, it is the right moment to share the insights of experience.

It is striking how the best strategies have been based on participation, building on good existing plans and processes, with clear attention to environment and development priorities. Conversely, failed strategies have tended to be prepared by small elite task forces without consultation, neglecting existing initiatives, and have been limited in scope. Experience shows you cannot deal with environmental issues without getting to the heart of development needs. National policy processes need to be linked with local planning and action. It is at the community level where many traditional and experimental participatory resource management approaches have borne fruit; but their sustainability remains constrained by poor policy environments. In the next few years, we may very well see the heart of critical decision-making moving closer to local levels — hence the importance of local strategies to harmonize local and national approaches. Finally, it is clear that the durable strategies arise from homespun demand. Political will is essential. No amount of heavy-handed conditionality leads to lasting results.

This handbook contains a wealth of material that we hope will be useful, not only in undertaking strategies, but for helping many other planning and programming approaches. It includes ideas for participation, financing for long-term processes, monitoring, donor roles, modes of cooperation, and so on.

Strategies are not simple exercises. They are very challenging. Their success depends, in most instances, on changed professional and institutional attitudes. We commend this document to governments, NGOs and donors in the hope that it will help foster a renaissance in planning and actions for a sustainable future.

Richard Sandbrook   David McDowell
Executive Director   Director General
IIED   IUCN

Preface

This handbook has been prepared as a collaborative activity between IUCN and IIED. It has involved members of the IUCN Commission on Environmental Strategies and Planning, specifically its Working Group on Strategies for Sustainability, and various members of the IUCN Secretariat, and of IIED, particularly its Environmental Planning Group. During the past two years, IUCN, through its field offices, has been working to establish regional networks of people with experience in strategies. Networks in Africa, Asia and Latin America have met a number of times and made important contributions to this handbook, which is one of a series being prepared by IUCN covering various types of strategies and associated methods for sustainable development. This handbook also draws heavily from material included in a series of strategy case studies prepared by the regional networks.

The process of preparing the handbook began in 1988 when IUCN held a workshop in Victoria Falls, Zimbabwe, to review the experience with national conservation strategies. More recently, members of the regional networks stressed the importance of such strategies and of sharing more widely the lessons of over a decade of strategy experience. Two network meetings were held in May 1992: one in Gland, Switzerland, the other in San José, Costa Rica, to set out a framework for the handbook and gather case study material. In November 1992, the Africa network met in Lake Baringo, Kenya, and the Asia network met in Air Keroh, Malaysia, to critically review an initial draft of the handbook and distil the key lessons learned.

In July 1993, the Africa network met again in Kenya as part of a broader meeting of IUCN Eastern African members, and the Latin America network met the same month in Isla Taboga, Panama. They discussed in more detail a handbook on local strategies and various strategy methods. The Asia network came together again in December 1993 in Delhi, India, to focus specifically on monitoring and evaluation; a follow-up meeting on this subject was held in Ottawa, Canada, in April 1994. Those meetings provided the final input to Chapter 9 on keeping strategies on track. They also reviewed the draft of a more detailed handbook on the assessment process, currently being prepared through a two-year programme of field testing.

This handbook reflects the strategy experience in Africa, Asia, Latin America and in a number of OECD countries. It does not specifically address Eastern Europe, although the lessons learned elsewhere are relevant to this region. At the time of the network meetings on which much of the analysis is based, the NEAP process and development of environment funds in Eastern Europe were in early stages. Now there is a rich experience in that region which needs to be shared through the other strategy networks worldwide, particularly as common problems of implementation, financing and monitoring are now being addressed.

Members of the IUCN regional networks who have been involved in the development of this handbook, either through their participation in network meetings, the preparation of case studies, or the provision of materials and comments on various drafts include:

Ramón Alvarado, A Anitha, Anil Agarwal, Ishak bin Ariffin, César Barrientos, Stephen Bender, Chitra Deo Bhatt, Robin Bidwell, Ben Boer, Max Börlin, Gerardo Budowski, Frank Bracho, Dulce M Cacha, Richard Carpenter, Juan-José Castro-Chamberlain, Ana Cazzadori, Sandhya Chatterji, Patrick M Chipungu, Alecky Chuprine, Barry Coates, Ralph Cobham, Cynthia Cook, Arthur Dahl, Geoffrey Davison, Jaime Echeverria, Tewolde Berhan G Egziabher, Margaret Evans, Patricia Fernandez, Alison Field-Juma, Vladimir Flint, Roberto Flores V, Tom Fox, Peter Freeman, Keith Garratt, George Greene, Wim Groen, Sterling Grogan, Arthur Hanson, Carlos Hernandez, Arthur Hoole, Saleemul Huq, Nadeem Ilahi, Anthony Judge, GMB Kariisa, Kerry ten Kate, George Khroda, Jerry Kozlowski, Bohumil Kucera, Hubert LeBlanc, Arturo López Ornat, Oscar Lücke, Toziri Lweno, Diego Lynch, Adolfo Mascarenhas, Andrea Matte-Baker, Juan Mayr, Lucia Merino, Ajay Mhotra, Lester Milbrath, Roger Morales, Victor Morgan, Margaret Mukahanana, David Munro, Fannie Mutepfa, John Naysmith, Kunzang Norbu, Silvio Olivieri, Ayo Olojede, Gene Owens, Jirí Pall, Drona Pkhrel, Carlos Quesada, Syed Ayub Qutub, James Ramsey, MS Ranatunga, Haroun Er Rashid, Walter Reid, Jennifer Reithbergen-McCracken, Carlos Rui Ribero, Arne Schiotz, José Arnoldo Sermeño Lima, Parmesh Shah, Anuradha Shrestha, Murray Silberman, David Simmons, Naresh Singh, Scott Slocombe, Stuart Stevenson, François Terrasson, Eduardo Trigo, Alex Trisoglio, Ted Trzyna, Frank Tugwell, Dan Tunstall, Karma Ura, Edmundo Vásquez, Robert Wabunoha, Ranjit Wijewansa, Brian Wilkes, and Adrian Wood.

Members of IUCN's Secretariat, either in field offices or headquarters, who have contributed in important ways, either as members of the networks or through their comment on drafts include:

Marcela Bonilla, Pierre Campredon, Anil Chitrakar, Michael Cockerell, Mark Dillenbeck, Danny Elder, Hans Friederich, Meghan Golay, Mark Halle, Martin Holdgate, John L Hough, Aban Marker Kabraji, Ram Khadka, John McEachearn, Jeff McNeely, Nancy

MacPherson, MM Maimbolwa, Peter-John Meynell, Allen Putney, Peter Sutcliffe, Sylvie Wabbes, and Leslie Wijesinghe.

One of the most important activities stemming from the discussions of the regional strategy networks is the IUCN programme currently under way in collaboration with IDRC, to develop frameworks for assessment of strategies so that they stick to their sustainable development goals. Chapter 9 draws from the initial phases of this work, which involves a special IUCN team, including: Ashoke Chatterjee, Eric Dudley, Tracey Goodman, Tony Hodge, Alejandro Imbach, Ashoke Khosla, Diana Lee-Smith, Adil Najam, Vijay Pillai and George C Varughese.

IIED staff members and associates who have made contributions at various times during the drafting process include:

Bruce Aylward, Ed Barbier, Josh Bishop, Michael Carley, Julian Lewis, Diana Mitlin, Jules Pretty, Nick Robins, Barry Sadler, Richard Sandbrook, David Satterthwaite, Bryan Spooner, John Thompson, Koy Thomson and Camilla Toulmin.

This handbook was written by an IUCN/IIED team consisting of Jeremy Carew-Reid, Robert Prescott-Allen, Stephen Bass and Barry Dalal-Clayton.

IIED's contribution was assisted by funding from the Norwegian Ministry of Foreign Affairs and the Overseas Development Administration of the UK. IUCN's contribution was assisted by the Canadian International Development Agency (CIDA), the International Development Research Centre (IDRC) of Canada, the United Nations Development Programme (UNDP) and the Swedish International Development Authority (SIDA) through its programme contribution to IUCN.

Publication of this handbook was supported by the UK ODA, UNDP and CIDA.

Overview

Learning from experience

In 1980, the World Conservation Strategy (WCS) recommended that countries undertake national and sub-national conservation strategies. Since then, hundreds of countries and communities have developed and implemented strategies. Some have been inspired by the WCS, others by Our Common Future (1987), still others by Caring for the Earth (1991) and Agenda 21 (1992). Some have been motivated or assisted by international organizations such as the World Bank, UNSO, UNDP, FAO, IIED, WRI and IUCN. Others have acted on their own initiative or relied entirely on their own resources. Reflecting their different histories, the strategies go by various names: conservation strategy, environmental action plan, environmental management plan, environmental policy plan, sustainable development strategy, national Agenda 21, and so on. They are referred to here by the umbrella term of 'strategies for sustainability'. Diverse though they are, the more successful strategies have common features, and lessons can be learned from them all. Chapter 2 summarizes 10 lessons from 14 years of experience with strategies for sustainability. We refer to them regularly throughout the handbook.

The contribution of strategies to sustainable development

Sustainable development means improving and maintaining the well-being of people and ecosystems. This goal is far from being achieved. It entails integrating economic, social and environmental objectives, and making choices among them where integration is not possible. People need to improve their relationships with each other and with the ecosystems that support them, by changing or strengthening their values, knowledge, technologies and institutions.

Major obstacles include lack of agreement on what should be done, resistance by interest groups who feel threatened by change, and uncertainty about the costs and benefits of alternatives. Overcoming these obstacles requires continuing public discussion, negotiation and mediation among interest groups, and development of a political consensus.

National sustainable development strategies (NSDSs) are needed to provide a framework for analysis and a focus for debate on sustainable development and processes of negotiation, mediation, and consensus-building, and to plan and carry out actions to change or strengthen values, knowledge, technologies and institutions with respect to priority issues.

Strategies can help countries solve inter-related economic, social and environmental problems by developing their capacities to treat them in an integrated fashion. Existing strategies have already resulted in improved organizations, procedures, legislation, public awareness and consensus on issues. Hence an existing strategic initiative – such as a national development plan, national conservation strategy, environmental action plan, or sectoral strategy – could be built into a national sustainable development strategy. Only in exceptional circumstances will an NSDS need to start from scratch.

Strategies are not panaceas, however. They are breaking new ground in the ways societies and governments tackle complex issues. Therefore, they can be controversial, take time to develop and get results, and require special management skills. They can too easily be marginalized because of the scope of the challenges they face. This handbook aims to help strategy participants and managers overcome such difficulties, and design and implement a successful strategy for sustainable development.

Building a national sustainable development strategy

Strategies may be international, national or local. They may be sectoral or multi-sectoral. This handbook covers national multi-sectoral strategies. In many countries, economic, social and environmental strategies are uncoordinated, each being undertaken parallel to the other. The number of partially integrated strategies is growing as environment strategies address economic and social concerns; and as development plans pay more attention to environmental factors. Although integration is increasing, no fully integrated sustainable development strategy yet exists.

The conditions required before developing a multi-sectoral national strategy include:

- a defined need and purpose;
- a location for the strategy's steering committee and secretariat where they can have the greatest influence on the national development system;
- high level support;
- the commitment of key participants; and
- a conducive political and social climate.

Necessary conditions that can be generated during the strategy process include:

- wide understanding of the concepts of sustainable development and the strategy, and of the need for both;
- clear goals and objectives;
- a broadly representative body of well-trained, experienced and committed people to drive the strategy;
- adequate resources; and
- effective communications.

Many of these conditions can more readily be developed by working on a strategy that is less ambitious than an NSDS, such as a sectoral, regional or local strategy.

The feasibility and scope of an NSDS can be determined by assessing whether the conditions can be met (and how to meet them), where change is most needed, how the strategy would relate to the decision-making system, how existing strategic processes could best be enhanced, what resources the strategy would need, and how they could be provided.

Participation in strategies

Sustainable development involves trade-offs among economic, social and ecological objectives. Such concessions cannot be determined by 'scientific' means alone, no matter how multi-disciplinary. They are value judgements, and therefore 'people-centred' approaches to sustainable development strategies are needed as well. Participation by stakeholder groups is critical for decision-making, and for all tasks of the strategy cycle, taking different forms for each task. The result will be a realistic strategy, with a broad base of knowledge, understanding and commitment from the groups involved, and with strong links to promising local initiatives.

The challenge of participation is considerable. 'Horizontal' participation across sectors and geographic regions has to be complemented by 'vertical' participation from national to local levels. It is best to begin by using existing structures and methods for participation, although they are usually weak. The introduction of new elements – participatory inquiry, communications/information and education campaigns, round tables and special committees – can have a great impact and is relatively easy. NGOs and local governments can help to bring this about. However, it is a mistake to think that participation is entirely a non-governmental affair; ultimately, governments need to find appropriate roles as facilitators in participation, and hence to continually increase the effectiveness of strategies.

Getting started

NSDSs need to build on, and provide a frame-work for, other forms of strategic processes operating at national level.

The strategy process should include:

- information assembly and analysis;
- policy formulation;
- action planning;
- implementation and
- monitoring and evaluation.

Each of these components is driven and facilitated by participation and communications. A multi-track process, whereby most of the strategy components occur simultaneously, is likely to be more effective than a single-track process, with most occurring sequentially. The strategy experience to date has usually followed a sequential approach without fully appreciating the central functions of communications and participation, or the importance of early implementation. A multi-track process, including working links between the various components and continual reflection and revision, inevitably will demand a broader range of management skills than the more conventional approach.

The basic management structure for most strategies has comprised a steering committee and secretariat. Although they have come in many shapes and sizes, experience suggests some general rules for their functions, location, status and composition. The start-up phase of a strategy can be a time of some frustration while relationships with existing activities are thought through, key participants brought on board (including financing and assistance bodies), decisions are made and the basic directions set from a range of options. Well-targeted, decisive but diplomatic management at this early stage can determine the level of success of the strategy in later phases.

Planning the strategy

A strategy is more likely to be implemented successfully if it concentrates on a few priority issues while retaining a broad purview.

The issues should be central to maintaining or improving the well-being of a significant proportion of a country's people and ecosystems and to achieving agreed economic objectives. They should be sufficiently high-profile and able to be tackled effectively to generate political support for the strategy. And the strategy should be able to make a clear difference in how the decision-making system deals with the issue.

A few broad but well-defined and measurable objectives are necessary for each issue, to enable monitoring and evaluation of the strategy and ensure it gets results. Participants analyse the issues to reach agreement on the objectives, and on the policies and actions required. This includes preparing a policy framework as well as specific cross-sectoral and sectoral policies. The policy framework should relate the strategy policy to the other policies of government (and of other participants in the strategy), identifying which policies may override it – and the circumstances under which they may do so – and which are subordinate. The last of the basic elements in planning a strategy is clearly defining the actions needed to put the policies into effect.

Implementing the strategy

The sooner implementation begins, the sooner the strategy can benefit from experience. Early action generates greater commitment and momentum to the process and builds capacities for managing it. Other plans for action will be needed, throughout government and at local levels. These include implementation by government, the private sector and NGOs. Each has a key function which can be helped through the appropriate legal frameworks, economic instruments and mechanisms for mediation and conflict resolution. Cooperation, rather than compulsion, is a useful rule of thumb.

The strategy secretariat, or the body which takes up its functions, has a key role to play, particularly through demonstration and pilot programmes bridging a number of sectors. Responsibility for implementation becomes more diffuse with each turn of the strategy cycle and as the institutional mechanisms for sustainable development mature. These will include new forms of partnership that emphasize flexibility and adaptable approaches to problem-solving and consensus-building.

Keeping strategies on track

There are significant challenges to be faced in the assessment tasks of strategies because they cover multiple sectors, geographical areas, objectives and actors.

Assessment combines monitoring, evaluating and reporting on the strategy. Assessment is primarily forward-looking. Its purpose is to improve the strategy process, help it meet objectives, and adapt the strategy to changing needs.

Assessment should be an integral part of the strategy from the start and cover all aspects: objectives, participation, communication, role in the decision-making system, planning, implementation, and results. Clear distinctions need to be made between assessing these strategy tasks themselves (a management function), assessing the changes in the broader environment in which the strategy operates, and assessing the impacts of the strategy. Careful choice of a manageable set of indicators is required for each.

Financing strategies and the role of external agencies

Funding agencies have played a crucial role in the development of national strategies, and there are now many lessons which can go to improving the important contribution such agencies have to make. Among them is the pressing need for donor coordination, so that the capacities of recipient communities are not undermined or distracted by overlapping and sometimes conflicting demands. There has been a tendency for donors to pick and choose from a portfolio of proposed actions. As a result, the strategy loses its importance as a framework for sustainable development. Donor support has been patchy, both in terms of the range of actions supported and of consistency of backing over time. Defining approaches for greater financial security needs to be given high priority.

National Environment Funds (NEFs) can contribute to long-term stable financing for strategies. Because NEFs rely on participatory management approaches, they also engender greater local control and self-reliance in the strategy process. One of the most attractive features of an NEF is its ability to distribute funding consistently over a long period of time at levels that local institutions can effectively absorb.

Like external funding support, technical assistance to national strategies from international organizations has produced mixed results. There are important lessons on how to use expatriate personnel. Experience has shown that international NGOs in particular can continue to play a vital role in providing the appropriate kinds of technical support to strategy teams.

No matter how successful some national strategies have been in attracting funds for their planning and implementation, the levels of resources are insignificant when compared to those associated with the big forces shaping development, such as structural adjustment policies and World Bank loans. The most important task for NSDSs for the remainder of the decade will be to harness and modify those forces to be consistent with sustainable development goals.

PART 1

An Approach to National Strategies

Chapter 1

How This Handbook Can Help

This handbook is intended for practitioners: people who are or expect to be involved in developing and implementing NSDSs or other multi-sectoral national strategies. Its aim is to help them improve and build on existing strategies or start one if none exist. Its advice is based on an analysis of past and current practice, drawing directly from the experience of practitioners of many strategic approaches.

The handbook does not suggest conformation to a single model: each strategy should be designed and run by the government and citizens of the country concerned.

The handbook is not an instruction manual. Users are recommended to study it and reflect on its implications for their own circumstances, and then to design an approach suitable for local purposes, conditions and available resources. We strongly encourage implementation of existing multi-sectoral strategies. They may be narrower in scope and less ambitious than an NSDS, but any improvements needed can be introduced concurrently with implementation.

Purpose of the handbook

This handbook is intended for practitioners – people in governments, citizens' and community groups, educational institutions, businesses and international organizations – who are or could be involved in developing and implementing a multi-sectoral strategy on environment and development at the national or provincial level.

The handbook describes how to use multi-sectoral strategies to integrate environmental, economic and social concerns in national development processes. It aims to help improve the usefulness and effectiveness of all such strategies: national sustainable development strategies (NSDSs), national conservation strategies (NCSs), national environmental action plans (NEAPs), and others.

The handbook suggests ways of developing and implementing an NSDS, either by building on an existing strategy or, if none exist, from scratch. Difficulties have been encountered with existing strategies because their scope is broad and they involve many different sectors and interests. Strategies are complex processes, and managing them is logistically demanding. Although similar to existing strategies in many ways, NSDS processes are likely to be even more challenging. Their scope is wider, and their task of combining economic, environmental and social concerns will increase their technical

complexity, the extent of participation required, and hence their political profile.

At the same time, the development and implementation of strategies whose focus is largely environmental – such as most NCSs and NEAPs – will continue to be important. The handbook's discussion of how to organize and manage strategies applies to these strategies as well as to the more ambitious NSDSs.

The handbook is based on an analysis of past and current practice, drawing directly from the experience of practitioners of many strategic approaches. It is a distillation of lessons learned from more than 60 national and provincial conservation strategies, environmental action plans, development plans and other multi-sectoral strategies in 50 upper- and lower-income countries since 1980. Case studies of some of these strategies have been published in IUCN's series of Regional Reviews of Strategies for Sustainability.

Many practitioners have contributed to the handbook by sharing their experience in workshops in Latin America, Africa, Asia and Europe. In so doing, they have helped develop the concept of strategies, raise standards, and propose ways of expanding their scope towards strategies for sustainable development.

Many of the methods described have been used successfully in current strategies. However, experience with strategies is evolving rapidly, and appropriate methods for some strategy elements have yet to be fully developed or tested. Some practices – for example, participatory inquiry – have been used successfully in other contexts and seem to hold promise for strategies as well. Other methods – for example, certain techniques of monitoring and evaluation – have not been tested, but are intended to meet needs recognized by a wide range of practitioners. Every strategy is to some extent experimental, and needs to be accompanied by research and monitoring.

Each country's strategy will be very different and will need to suit the nation's individual set of geographical, ecological, socio-cultural, economic and political conditions. Any form of straitjacket imposed by external agencies or conditions is inappropriate. This handbook does not suggest conformation to a single model: each strategy should be designed and run by the government and citizens of the country concerned.

How to use the handbook

The handbook presents principles and ideas on process and methods, and suggests how they can be used. It is not an instruction manual for a 'model' strategy for constant reference during the strategy process. Users are recommended to study the handbook, to consider its relevance and implications for their own circumstances, and then to design an approach suitable for local purposes, conditions and available resources.

We recommend reading every chapter in sequence for users who have not yet been involved in developing a strategy, are in the early stages of preparing a new strategy, or are considering revising an existing strategy to cover a more ambitious remit (for example, an NSDS). Other users may wish to concentrate on particular elements of the strategy process.

The handbook describes the main kinds of multi-sectoral national strategies. It suggests how to start a new strategy, as well as different ways to build on an existing strategy. It sets out essential conditions for an effective multi-sectoral strategy, ways of developing the required conditions, and alternative approaches if conditions remain unfavourable.

The handbook then provides guidance on the design and management of the strategy process, and on its main elements: participation, information assembly and analysis, policy formulation, action planning, implementation and capacity-building, communication, and monitoring and evaluation. This is the heart of the handbook, and should be useful for anyone who is actively engaged in planning, managing, or reviewing a national strategy process.

We strongly encourage implementation of existing multi-sectoral strategies. They may be narrower in scope and less ambitious than an NSDS, but any improvements needed can be introduced concurrently with implementation. It would be a mistake to postpone implementation by starting another process or preparing another document. The intention of this handbook is not to undermine any existing strategic process, but to show ways in which it can be strengthened and made more effective.

Chapter 2

Ten Lessons and Features for Success

In 1980, the World Conservation Strategy (WCS) (IUCN/UNEP/WWF 1980) recommended that countries undertake national and subnational conservation strategies. Since then, hundreds of countries and communities have developed and implemented strategies. Some have been inspired by the WCS, others by Our Common Future (WCED 1987), still others by Caring for the Earth (IUCN/UNEP/WWF 1991) and Agenda 21 (UNCED 1992). Some have been motivated or assisted by international organizations, such as the World Bank, UNSO, UNDP, IIED, WRI and IUCN. Others have acted on their own initiative or relied entirely on their own resources.

Reflecting their different histories, the strategies go by various names: conservation strategy, environmental action plan, environmental management plan, environmental policy plan, sustainable development strategy, national Agenda 21, and so on. They are referred to here by the umbrella term of 'strategies for sustainability'. Diverse though they are, the more successful strategies have common features, and lessons can be learned from them all. Here, ten lessons from fourteen years of experience with strategies for sustainability are summarized. We return to them regularly throughout the handbook.

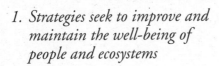

1. Strategies seek to improve and maintain the well-being of people and ecosystems

A strategy for sustainability is a process of:

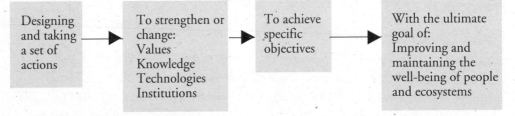

| Designing and taking a set of actions | → | To strengthen or change: Values Knowledge Technologies Institutions | → | To achieve specific objectives | → | With the ultimate goal of: Improving and maintaining the well-being of people and ecosystems |

2. The overall goal of strategies is sustainable development

Most strategies for sustainability have focused on environmental objectives. A few, such as Bhutan's Seventh Five-Year Plan, have mainly development objectives. But in all cases the ultimate goal is to improve the condition of both people and the ecosystems of which they are a part. This goal is variously described as sustainable development, sustainable living or sustainable well-being. It means that strategies have an important role as integrators of socio-economic and ecological perspectives and of the policies, plans and programmes of interacting sectors and interest groups.

3. The choice of strategy objectives should be tactical

With a broad goal such as sustainable development, it is tempting to try to do everything. But strategies with too many objectives can get bogged down, break up into a mess of projects, or reduce the objectives to those that are top priority.

Strategies need objectives that are:

- few enough to be achievable;
- encompassing enough to ensure the support of participants and prevent the strategy being fragmented and losing coherence; and
- clearly defined and measurable enough to assess progress.

4. The strategy process is adaptive and cyclical

A strategy is a process, not an isolated event. The process is adaptive; it develops as it goes along and responds to change. It is cyclical; over a period of several years, the main components are repeated. This means that a strategy need not and should not try to do everything at once. It can grow in scope, ambition and degree of participation as capacities to undertake the strategy are built. Pakistan, for example, started with a national conservation strategy and went on to develop provincial conservation strategies; Malaysia developed state strategies first and then a national strategy. Neither tried to develop national and subnational strategies at the same time.

5. The strategy should be as participatory as possible

Participation means sharing responsibility for the strategy and jointly undertaking it. The participants in a strategy should be those whose values, knowledge, technology or insti-tutions need to change or be strengthened to achieve the objectives. The objectives determine the participants and the participants decide the objectives. Participants bring information to the strategy, ensuring that it is based on a common understanding of purpose, problems and solutions. Participation is the most effective way of communicating the information on which the strategy is based, its objectives, and the actions to be taken. People who participate in designing and deciding actions are more likely to understand their purpose and to implement them in full.

Participation should be expanded as the strategy develops. Usually, the nature and extent of participation will vary with the type of strategy and how far it has evolved. In many national strategies, for example, local involvement is at first selective and focused on representative communities.

6. Communication is the lifeblood of a strategy

Communication is the means by which:

- participants exchange information with each other about values, perceptions, interests, ecosystems, resources, the economy and society;
- participants reach agreement with each other on actions;
- values are changed or strengthened and knowledge is imparted; and
- participants inform others about the strategy.

Therefore, communication needs to be planned carefully as an integral part of the strategy.

7. Strategies are processes of planning and action

Planning is an important part of a strategy, but a strategy is much more than a plan. It is a process of developing a long-term vision or sense of direction; targeting the key things that can be done to move in that direction (priority issues, key influences on those issues, and the most effective ways of dealing with them); and engaging everyone concerned – businesses, citizens' groups, communities, as well as governments – to carry them out.

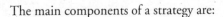

The main components of a strategy are:

- assessment, including diagnosis (survey, issue, identification and analysis at the start of a strategy) and monitoring and evaluation (during a strategy);
- designing the actions (planning); and
- taking the actions (implementation).

These components must continue together and reinforce one another. Most strategies have begun by working in sequence: diagnosis first; then planning; then implementation. But this need not be the case. It is better that implementation, for example, starts early; it does not have to wait for all planning to be completed. Once the strategy is underway, implementation and monitoring should be continuous. Evaluation and the planning of new actions should be repeated at intervals; for example, every three to five years.

Monitoring and evaluation are vital for success; keeping the strategy on course and enabling it to adapt to changing conditions and results. Evaluation needs to focus on how the strategy is carried out as well as on the results.

Although many strategies are called 'plans' rather than 'strategies' – and many strategies started out as plans – all effective strategies are action-oriented and have gone well beyond planning. For example, the Dutch National Environmental Policy Plan has become an instrument for structural change

in production and consumption, with interest groups, sectors and corporations committing themselves to change their behaviour to meet agreed targets. The Seychelles used its National Environment Management Plan to establish the institutional framework for sustainable development, including a Ministry of Environment, Economic Planning and External Relations.

Therefore, it is best to think of a strategy not as a plan but as a means of planning and taking actions to change or strengthen values, knowledge, technologies and institutions. By the same token, a strategy document is an essential tool to make the strategy explicit and record the policies and actions agreed by the participants. But it is only a tool; it is not the strategy. Too great an emphasis on preparing a document can divert energy from the actions the document is meant to promote.

8. Integrate the strategy into the decision-making systems of society

Strategies should be integrated with conventional development cycles; they are not just something to be added on. In Ethiopia and Pakistan, for example, the national conservation strategies are expected by government and donors to act as the strategic framework for all development investment and actions.

The strategy should build on priority areas where government and people are already committed. Politicians and communities need to see its benefits and relevance. It should draw on local knowledge, values, skills and intuitions.

The strategy should also build on past or current plans rather than ignore or replace them. It should recognize and capture the best of what is available and has already been done.

9. Build the capacity to undertake a strategy at the earliest stage

At a national level, this means building the capacity for cross-sectoral action, finding ways of integrating environmental concerns with development, and developing processes to alert government agencies and the private sector about their environmental responsi-bilities. In the Nepal NCS, this has been done by training key technical staff from various ministries in environmental impact assessment, an activity that led to environ-mental units being set up in key ministries and an Environmental Protection Council.

10. External agencies should be 'on tap', not on top

External financial and technical assistance should help the society concerned increase its capacity to undertake strategies for sustainabil-ity. Recipient governments must be able to take the lead in coordinating assistance. Locally-designed and locally-driven approaches to strategies should be given precedence over conditions on aid or notions of 'model' strategies. Low-level continuous support over a long period is almost always better than high-level support for a limited period. Donors should support the capacity-building process and not just the products of the strategy. Their support for implementation should include refocusing existing investments as well as new investment.

Box 1: Ten lessons and features of national strategies for sustainability

1. They seek to improve and maintain the well-being of people and ecosystems.
2. Their overall goal is sustainable development.
3. Their objectives are strategic and tactical.
4. The process is adaptive and cyclical.
5. They are participatory.
6. They rely on communication.
7. They are processes of planning and action.
8. They are integrative and inter-sectoral.
9. They build capacity.
10. External agencies should be on tap, not on top.

Definition: Strategies for sustainability are processes of planning and action to improve and maintain the well-being of people and ecosystems.

Chapter 3

The Contribution of Strategies to Sustainable Development

Sustainable development means improving and maintaining the well-being of people and ecosystems. This goal is far from being achieved. To develop sustainably, people need to improve their relationships with each other and with the ecosystems that support them – by changing or strengthening their values, knowledge, technologies and institutions.

Major obstacles include a lack of agreement on what should be done, resistance by interest groups who feel threatened by change, and uncertainty about the costs and benefits of alternatives. Overcoming these obstacles requires continuing public discussion, negotiation and mediation among interest groups, and development of a political consensus.

National sustainable development strategies are needed to provide a framework and focus for debate on sustainable development and processes of negotiation, mediation, and consensus-building; and to plan and carry out actions to change or strengthen values, knowledge, technologies and institutions with respect to priority issues. An existing strategic initiative, such as a national development plan, national conservation strategy, environmental action plan, or sectoral strategy, could be built into a national sustainable development strategy.

Strategies can help countries solve inter-related economic, social and environmental problems by developing their capacities to treat them in an integrated fashion. Existing strategies have already resulted in improved organizations, procedures, legislation, public awareness and consensus on issues.

Strategies are not panaceas, however. They are breaking new ground in the ways societies and governments tackle complex issues. Therefore, they can be controversial, take time to develop and get results, and require special management skills. This handbook aims to help strategy participants and managers overcome such difficulties, and design and implement a successful strategy for sustainable development.

The challenge of sustainable development

Over the past 30 years, growing numbers of people have come to recognize that efforts to improve their standard of living must be in harmony with the natural world. Many have also realized that a lack of development can be as great a threat to nature as reckless or misguided development.

The idea that conservation and development are two sides of the same coin became current in the 1970s. The World Conservation Strategy (IUCN/WWF/UNEP 1980) called for the integration of conservation and development:

'...because unless patterns of development that also conserve living resources are widely adopted, it will become impossible to meet the needs of today without foreclosing the achievement of tomorrow's.'

The World Conservation Strategy called development that is sustained by conservation 'sustainable development': a term that in 1987 was taken up and widely publicized by the Brundtland Commission's report, Our Common Future (WCED 1987). Since then, people have struggled with what sustainable development means in practice, and how to achieve it. They have wrestled with the meanings of 'sustainable' and 'development'. Some have proposed rival terms, such as 'ecologically sustainable development', 'ethical and sustainable development', 'sustainable living' and 'sustainable well-being'.

Regardless of terminology, the central concept is the same; the human system is an integral part of the ecosystem. A society is sustainable only if both the human condition and the condition of the ecosystem are satisfactory or improving (Box 2). If either is unsatisfactory or worsening, the society is unsustainable.

Human and ecosystem well-being

Hence, sustainable development (or sustainable living or sustainable well-being) entails improving and maintaining the well-being of people and ecosystems.

Human well-being exists if all members of society are able to define and meet their needs and have a large range of choices and opportunities to fulfill their potential.

Ecosystem well-being means ecosystems maintain their quality and diversity and thus their potential to adapt to change and provide a wide range of options for the future.

In most societies today, neither condition is being met. In some, progress is being made in one area at the expense of the other. Even in wealthy societies, which make huge demands on resources and the environment,

Box 2: *The twin pillars of sustainable development*

The twin pillars of sustainable development are respect and concern for people and ecosystems. Development is likely to be sustainable if:

1. It improves the quality of human life. The purpose of development is to improve the quality of human life. It should enable people to realize their potential and lead lives of dignity and fulfillment. Economic growth is part of development, but it cannot be a goal in itself; nor can it go on indefinitely. Although people differ in their goals for development, some are virtually universal: a long and healthy life, education, access to resources needed for a decent standard of living, political freedom, guaranteed human rights, and freedom from violence. Development is achieved only if it makes lives better in all these respects.

2. It conserves the Earth's vitality and diversity. Development must be conservation-based: it must protect the structure, functions and diversity of the world's natural systems on which our species depends. To this end we need to:

- Conserve life-support systems. These are the ecological processes that shape climate, cleanse air and water, regulate water flow, recycle essential elements, create and regenerate soil, enable ecosystems to renew themselves, and keep the planet fit for life.
- Conserve biological diversity, including all species of plants, animals and other organisms, the range of genetic stocks within species, and the variety of ecosystems.
- Ensure that all uses of renewable resources are sustainable. These resources include soil, wild and domesticated organisms, forests, rangelands, farmlands, and the marine and freshwater ecosystems that support fisheries. A use is likely to be sustainable if it is compatible with maintaining the viability of the species and ecosystems affected by the use.
- Minimize the depletion of non-renewable resources, such as minerals, oil, gas and coal, which cannot be used sustainably in the same sense as plants, fish or soil. But their 'life' can and should be extended; by recycling, by using less of a resource to make a particular product, or by switching to renewable substitutes where possible.
- Keep within the Earth's carrying capacity. There are finite limits to the capacity of ecosystems and to the impacts that they and the Earth as a whole can withstand without dangerous deterioration. Limits vary from region to region, and the impacts depend on how many people there are and how much food, water, energy and raw material each person uses or wastes. A few people consuming a lot can cause as much damage as a lot of people consuming a little. Policies, technologies and practices that bring human numbers and lifestyles into balance with the Earth's carrying capacity are essential.

Source: IUCN/WWF/UNEP (1991).

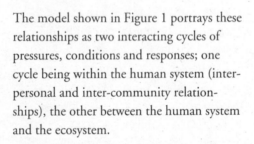
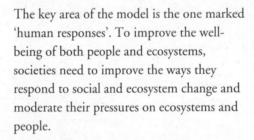
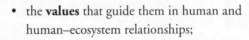

there can be extreme poverty and social decay among the least advantaged. This widespread evidence of unsustainability is summarized in Box 3.

Two sets of relationships are crucial to improving the well-being of people and ecosystems:

- human relationships, both inter-personal (among individuals and families) and inter-community (among communities, organizations and nations); and
- relationships between people and the ecosystem.

The model shown in Figure 1 portrays these relationships as two interacting cycles of pressures, conditions and responses; one cycle being within the human system (inter-personal and inter-community relation-ships), the other between the human system and the ecosystem.

The key area of the model is the one marked 'human responses'. To improve the well-being of both people and ecosystems, societies need to improve the ways they respond to social and ecosystem change and moderate their pressures on ecosystems and people.

Specifically, societies need to change or strengthen:

- the **values** that guide them in human and human–ecosystem relationships;

- the **knowledge** that enables them to understand and make sense of these relationships;
- the **technologies** with which they apply their knowledge and equip themselves with tools and infrastructure; and
- the institutions – the customs, laws, social and economic incentives, and organizations – by which they manage the relationships.

Values

Values based on respect and care for each other and the Earth are the foundation for a sustainable society. The transition to sustainability will require changes in how people perceive each other and other life on Earth, how they evaluate their needs and priorities, and how they behave. Values are important because what people do depends on what they believe. Widely-shared beliefs are often more powerful than government edicts.

Values that emphasize respect and concern for people and respect and concern for ecosystems can be found in many religions and cultures and in basic global statements such as the Universal Declaration of Human Rights (UN 1948), the World Charter for Nature (UN 1982), and the Rio Declaration (UN 1992). Seldom, however, are the values expressed in such declarations, or embraced by religions or cultures, manifest at ground levels.

Box 3: Signs of unsustainability

Rising human numbers and consumption of resources: Since the industrial revolution, human numbers have grown eightfold. Water withdrawals have grown from 100 to 3600 cubic kilometres a year. The 5.3 billion people now on the Earth use 40 per cent of its most elemental resource: the energy from the sun made available by green plants on land.

Poverty: More than a billion people live in absolute poverty. One person in five cannot get enough food to support an active working life. One quarter of the world's people are without safe drinking water. Every year millions of children die from malnutrition and preventable disease.

Resource depletion: In less than 200 years, the planet has lost six million square kilometres of forest. An estimated 60,000–70,000 square kilometres of agricultural land is made unproductive by erosion each year. The sediment load from soil erosion has risen threefold in major river basins and by eight times in smaller, more intensively used ones.

Pollution: Human inputs of nutrients into coastal waters already equal natural sources. Human-caused emissions of many heavy metals now range from double those from natural sources (for example, arsenic and mercury) to five and even 18 times higher than natural rates (cadmium and lead respectively).

Global climate change: The climate regime to which people and other forms of life have long been adapted is threatened by human impact on the atmosphere. Since the mid-18th century, human activities have more than doubled the methane in the atmosphere, increased the concentration of carbon dioxide by 27 per cent, and significantly damaged the stratospheric ozone layer.

Debt: The combined cumulative debt of lower-income countries is more than $1 trillion, and interest payments alone have reached $60 billion per year. As a result, since 1984 there has been a net transfer of capital from lower-income to upper-income countries. Nonetheless, many upper-income countries also run substantial deficits.

Source: IUCN/UNEP/WWF (1991).

Figure 1: Relationships between people and the Earth

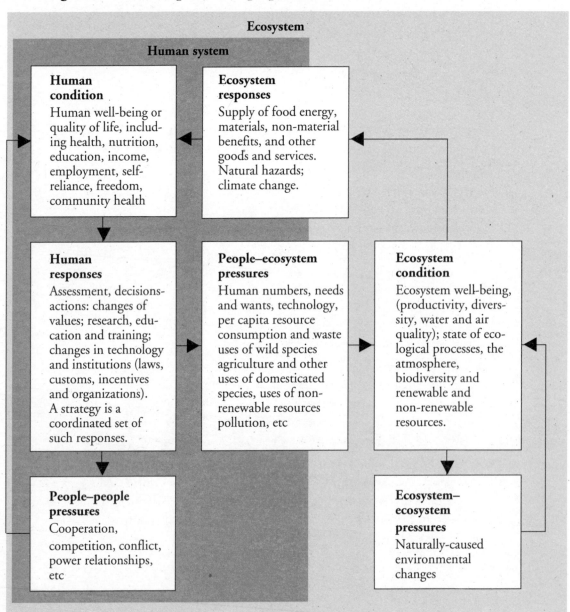

Ecosystem

Human system

Human condition
Human well-being or quality of life, including health, nutrition, education, income, employment, self-reliance, freedom, community health

Ecosystem responses
Supply of food energy, materials, non-material benefits, and other goods and services. Natural hazards; climate change.

Human responses
Assessment, decisions-actions: changes of values; research, education and training; changes in technology and institutions (laws, customs, incentives and organizations). A strategy is a coordinated set of such responses.

People–ecosystem pressures
Human numbers, needs and wants, technology, per capita resource consumption and waste uses of wild species agriculture and other uses of domesticated species, uses of non-renewable resources pollution, etc

Ecosystem condition
Ecosystem well-being, (productivity, diversity, water and air quality); state of ecological processes, the atmosphere, biodiversity and renewable and non-renewable resources.

People–people pressures
Cooperation, competition, conflict, power relationships, etc

Ecosystem–ecosystem pressures
Naturally-caused environmental changes

Notes: a) The human system is a part of the ecosystem.

b) Relationships crucial to the well-being of people and ecosystems are portrayed as two interacting cycles of pressures, conditions and responses — one cycle within the human system, the other between the human system and the ecosystem.

There are many reasons why people live unsustainably. People who are poor are often forced to do things to help them survive for the present that they know create problems for the future. The more affluent live unsustainably because of ignorance, lack of concern, or incentives to wasteful consumption.

People will adopt attitudes and practices more conducive to sustainable development when they are persuaded that it is right and necessary, when they have sufficient incentive, and when they can obtain the required knowledge and skills. Societies must provide incentives, formal and informal education and training to promote values that support a sustainable way of life and discourage values that are incompatible with it.

Knowledge

There is a lack of scientific information and an inadequate understanding of ecosystem functions. This means that development often proceeds in ignorance of the possible consequences, and with no or inadequate measures taken to avoid or counter negative environmental effects. Predicting the effects of human activities is difficult, and continuous monitoring of vulnerable ecosystems is essential. Direct cause and effect are often far from obvious and are the subject of disagreement among scientists. Political and economic change at all levels, from international to local, add to the uncertainty. But the problems are too big and the consequences of delay too serious to risk inaction until there is scientific certainty. In any case, given the many variables, scientific certainty is most unlikely.

Environmental, social and economic problems are complex. Their interactions are hard to detect and change constantly. A wide range of scientific, economic, political and philosophical knowledge and skills is needed to understand and resolve them.

Understanding ecosystems, societies and their relationships therefore needs constant improvement through research. Existing information on these relationships should be made more accessible and useful through synthesis and analysis, which should be widely communicated and incorporated in education and training programmes.

Technologies

Technologies provide people with tools and infrastructure: a means of communication, transportation, energy supply and use, water supply, waste disposal, and extraction of raw materials and their manufacture into products. Research and development are needed, as well as better manufacturing, engineering and physical planning processes, in order to develop and apply technologies that:

- minimize hazards to people and ecosystems; and
- minimize the use of energy and raw materials, reduce waste, and prevent pollution.

Institutions

Laws and incentives

Laws and incentives are necessary to ensure that people and their organizations behave sustainably. But existing legislation and incentives do not provide adequately for sustainability, and often the two systems conflict with each other. For example, the law may tell a business not to pollute a river, but more powerful economic incentives may encourage it to do so.

At present, incentives to deplete resources and degrade ecosystems are strong because the market treats ecosystems and their functions as useless, limitless or free of charge. The market does not take account of the full value of ecological processes or biodiversity, or of the costs borne by society when these values are degraded.

Comprehensive and effective legal frameworks are needed to safeguard human rights, the interests of future generations, and the vitality and diversity of ecosystems; and incentive systems should be in harmony with them.

Organizations

In many countries, governmental planning and decision-making systems are weak compared with financial and commercial interests. Some are excessively bureaucratic; many are insufficiently participatory to reflect the interests of local communities or the poor. Other organizational problems include limited political awareness of the social and ecological aspects of sustainable development, insufficient skilled personnel and lack of money. All such problems are closely related, and are exacerbated by each other, as well as by other problems such as inadequate legislative frameworks and lack of scientific information.

Traditionally, development planners have concentrated on controlling the allocation of resources to promote economic growth. Planning horizons have tended to be short: typically three to five years. In general, environmental and social concerns have been subordinated to crude measures of economic performance such as gross domestic product (GDP), employment generation, and foreign exchange earnings.

Development policies – particularly sectoral plans and annual budgetary processes – are usually given priority over environmental policies. Both are fragmented and poorly integrated with each other. In some countries, national planning focuses excessively on projects, particularly large-scale projects, rather than on the institutions and programmes needed for sustainable development. Or, project plans may entail major policy decisions for which the national plan provides no guidance or which override the national plan. Often there is a poor fit among national, regional and local decision-making and powers to act.

Miscommunication, gaps, overlap and conflicts among sectors are common. This lack of horizontal integration is most obvious:

- within economic development planning, notably between sectors;
- between development policies and plans and environmental policies and plans (partly due to the longer time scale of the latter; and
- in the ways that it is made difficult for interest groups and the public to understand and affect development and environment decisions.

Mechanisms for integration are weak and usually only exist at lower levels of planning, such as regional or local land use plans. Environmental impact assessment (EIA), although important for identifying and preventing environmental and social problems, is applied to projects and programmes more often than to development plans, sectoral plans or policies. As such, it does not have 'upward reach': it can change or mitigate a project but is unlikely to alter the policy or plan that gives rise to the project.

Failures of economic planning and the rapid decline of central planning systems have led to proclamations of the supremacy of the market system. There is no doubt that the market system has been more successful than state planning at promoting enterprise, economic growth, and economic efficiency. But a healthy society is much more than an efficient economy. Many social and environmental objectives require some other mechanism than one designed to maximize utility or profits. Moreover, the market has been very poor at integrating environmental factors into economic decision-making. Such integration remains a central need.

Given the complexity and rapidly changing nature of economic, environmental and social problems, rigid bureaucratic structures are ineffective. Worse, they are likely to compound the problems; as are governments acting alone and, still more so, individual government agencies acting alone. In addition, politicians lack sufficient motivation to undertake the thankless task of mediating among conflicting economic, social and environmental objectives that diverge substantially from the status quo.

Today new forms of government are needed, with more flexible structures. Governments need to be organized to facilitate a greater flow of information and expertise among sectors – rather than just within single sectors – and between governmental and non-governmental entities.

Communities and local groups provide the most accessible channels for people to express their concerns and take action to create culturally-appropriate sustainable societies. To enable them to do this, communities need effective control over their own lives, including secure access to resources and an equitable share in managing them; the right

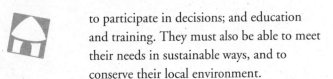

to participate in decisions; and education and training. They must also be able to meet their needs in sustainable ways, and to conserve their local environment.

Non-governmental organizations (NGOs) like environmental groups and social development groups have enormous potential to mobilize local and national energies toward sustainable development. They are already leading valuable efforts to combine socio-economic development and environmental conservation at the grassroots level. But too often they have been marginalized by both government and the market, lacking equitable arrangements to become partners in planning and decision-making.

One approach is for government agencies, communities, businesses and non-governmental interest groups to form partnerships or dynamic networks in which they work together to solve common problems in an integrated fashion. In so doing, they should take care to ensure that a network operating at one level (eg, community, provincial, national or international) coordinates with partnerships working on the same or a related issue at other levels.

Obstacles to change

Making the required changes to values, knowledge systems, technologies and institutions is fraught with difficulties.

- Lack of agreement on the existence and severity of the problems, how to resolve them, and who among nations and interest groups is responsible for doing so. Disagreement is inevitable, because the issues involve value judgements and because of the absence of scientific certainty.

- The systemic or structural nature of many of the problems. Problems such as poverty and inequalities within and among nations are not mere side-effects of the way we do business. They are deeply embedded in our institutions. Meeting basic needs will require changes in the distribution of wealth and control over resources. Achieving sustainability will require changes in the ways corporations and consumers use resources and generate waste. Powerful groups – from big corporations, governments and political parties to ordinary workers, consumers and voters – will try to block changes that they perceive to threaten their immediate interests. Only the threat of even worse change if the required action is not taken – and confidence that compensating benefits can be obtained in the near future – will overcome this resistance.

- Lack of a model of economic development that would provide an acceptable standard of living for all, and at the same time keep environmental impacts and uses of energy and raw materials within sustainable bounds. The industrial model of development is not a viable option. It has brought prosperity to only about 1.5 billion people – few in world terms – and its environmental costs have been huge. Even if the expected eventual world population of 10–12 billion people were able to industrialize, the impact on the planet would be catastrophic. Yet people and their governments are reluctant to try different ways of developing because the results are so uncertain. It is a case of 'better the devil you know than the devil you don't'.

Overcoming such obstacles calls for:

- Continuing public discussion of the nature of sustainable development, its ethical framework, and how to make the transition to sustainability, in order to develop a sense of common interest and a collective vision of the future.
- Negotiation and mediation. Decisions intended to lead to sustainability depend on value judgements: for example, the appropriate balance of short-term and long-term needs, or of industrial production and environmental quality. Such decisions involve difficult trade-offs between potentially conflicting objectives and different options. Often they have far-reaching consequences. Hence, they are essentially ethical and political and need to be negotiated among many sectors and interest groups.
- Development of a political consensus. Consensus does not mean unanimity or the absence of dissent: differing values

and perspectives are a fact of life. Nor does it mean the exclusion of minority concerns. Consensus means general agreement: a common understanding of what values are shared and how to behave when values conflict. The ultimate aim is to expand consensus to include all values necessary for sustainability and all interest groups.

The need for strategies

'National sustainable development strategies should be seen as a voyage and not as a harbour.'

Partnerships for Change Conference, Manchester, 1993

Strategies are needed to overcome the obstacles to sustainable development and make the necessary key changes. Haphazard or piecemeal attempts to do this are unlikely to succeed. The changes required are profound, and, to avoid doing more harm than good, will have to be made incrementally. But a process of incremental change is likely to lose direction without an explicit strategy to keep it on course.

It is not suggested that all of a nation's efforts toward sustainable development be entirely subsumed into one single strategy. Such a grand design is impractical and unnecessary. What is necessary is to provide the many actors involved with a sense of collective endeavour, a common (albeit evolving) conceptual framework, and a focus and energy source for a set of key initiatives.

National sustainable development strategies (NSDSs) are needed to:

- provide a forum and context for the debate on sustainable development and the articu-lation of a collective vision of the future;
- provide a framework for processes of negotiation, mediation, and consensus-building; and to focus them on a common set of priority issues;
- plan and carry out actions to change or strengthen values, knowledge, technologies and institutions with respect to the priority issues; and
- develop organizational capacities and other institutions required for sustainable development.

The purpose of NSDSs and other multi-sectoral strategies is to mobilize and focus a society's efforts to achieve sustainable development. National strategies for sustainability are participatory and cyclical processes of planning and action to achieve economic, ecological and social objectives in a balanced and integrated manner (Figure 2). NSDSs aim to achieve all three objectives; other strategies for sustainability emphasize one or two of them. The process, in most cases, encompasses the definition of policies and action plans, their implementation, monitoring and regular review.

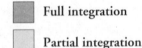

Figure 2: Sustainable development: integration of objectives

Economic objectives

Social objectives

Environmental objectives

■ Full integration

▢ Partial integration

Sustainable development will entail integration of economic, social and environmental objectives where possible, and making trade-offs among objectives where integration is not possible.

All countries probably have some kind of existing strategic initiative that can be built into an NSDS. This may be a national development plan, a national conservation strategy or an environmental action plan. It may be a strategy covering a sector such as forestry, agriculture or transport; or a theme such as biodiversity. A national strategy could also be built from several subnational strategies. Chapter 4 discusses how to start an NSDS or develop one from an existing initiative.

The role of strategies

The purpose of strategies for sustainability is to mobilize and focus a society's efforts to achieve sustainable development. They can do so by providing the means to:

- define choices, goals, targets and standards for sustainable development;
- illuminate the ethical dimensions underlying the choices and goals;
- analyze ecological, economic and social issues in a comprehensive and integrated fashion, clarifying links, exploring ethical considerations, identifying policy gaps, and showing how to reduce conflicts between environment and development;
- identify and evaluate options for addressing priority issues (problems and opportunities), which includes identifying appropriate packages of legal reforms, economic instruments, institutional development, capacity-building, and other programmes;
- prepare and carry out sectoral and cross-sectoral policies and plans to rationalize responsibilities for environment and development, reduce duplication, close gaps, prevent or reduce conflicts, and take advantage of compatibilities and synergies among sectors and interest groups;

- improve decision-making through better information and analytical techniques, and by enabling those most affected by decisions to contribute to them;
- develop understanding and build consensus so that decisions have strong support;
- identify, promote and support actions leading to sustainable development and reduce, slow or stop actions impeding sustainable development;
- identify and apply practices to sustain the resource base of the economy, achieve sustainable levels of resource use, restore degraded natural resources, make use of unused or under-used resource potential, improve the efficiency of existing resource use, and diversify the use of existing resources;
- determine priorities for action, evaluating costs and benefits and the trade-offs between the often very different concerns affecting society;
- allocate limited resources;
- develop and strengthen institutions for sustainable development; and
- build capacities to handle complex and inter-related issues.

National sustainable development strategies are gaining recognition as a highly appropriate course of action for many countries. This was highlighted both in Caring for the Earth (IUCN/UNEP/WWF 1991) and in Agenda 21 (UNCED 1992) (see Box 4):

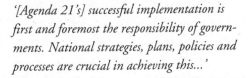

'[Agenda 21's] successful implementation is first and foremost the responsibility of governments. National strategies, plans, policies and processes are crucial in achieving this...'

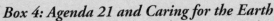

Governments – in cooperation, where appropriate, with international organizations – should adopt an NSDS based on, among other things, the implementation of

decisions taken at UNCED in 1992, particularly in respect of Agenda 21. This strategy should build upon and harmonize the various sectoral economic, social and environmental policies and plans that are operating in the country. The experience gained through existing planning exercises such as national reports for UNCED, national conservation strategies and

Box 4: Agenda 21 and Caring for the Earth

Agenda 21 is the action plan of the United Nations Conference on Environment and Development (UNCED, Rio de Janeiro, 1992), agreed to by 178 governments. Other UNCED agreements were the Climate and Biodiversity Conventions, the Forest Principles, and the Rio Declaration. The 40 chapters of the Agenda 21 document cover a great many issues relating to sustainable development, including developing the organization, skills and resources required for implementation. Its actions are to be undertaken at all levels, from the local to the international. Agenda 21 attempts to integrate environment and development, identify links among sectors, and examine cross-sectoral issues such as poverty, consumption, and financial resources.

Agenda 21 is not legally binding, but it does represent political commitment at the highest level. A recent survey of 81 countries showed that 65 of them had designated organizations to oversee implementation of Agenda 21. All United Nations' agencies are responding to Agenda 21.

Caring for the Earth is a global strategy for sustainable living, prepared by the World Conservation Union, the United Nations Environment Programme, and the World Wide Fund for Nature. It builds on the World Conservation Strategy (IUCN/UNEP/WWF 1980), continuing the emphasis on conserving the Earth's vitality and diversity, while adding an ethical dimension and proposing actions to improve the quality of human life, keep within the Earth's carrying capacity, and integrate development and conservation at individual, community, national and global levels. Caring for the Earth contributed to, and complements, Agenda 21. The two could well be used together.

Those chapters of Agenda 21 and Caring for the Earth which are particularly relevant to a discussion of NSDSs are listed at the end of this chapter.

environment action plans should be fully used and incorporated into a country-driven sustainable development strategy. Its goals should be to ensure socially responsible economic development while protecting the resource base and the environment for the benefit of future generations. It should be developed through the widest possible participation.

The benefits of strategies

Some countries undertake strategies for sustainability when they begin to recognize that ad hoc and piecemeal attempts to solve environment and development problems are not working. The problems may be resource depletion; erosion, pollution and other forms of environmental degradation; loss of natural habitats; increased competition for land; rising levels of friction among resource users; frustration of social or economic objectives; or rejection of decisions by groups who feel excluded from decision-making.

Strategies have a number of strengths. Their integrated multi-sectoral approach should enable countries to act on the basis of a better understanding of how environmental, social and economic problems relate to each other. Strategies can stimulate and focus cross-sectoral debate, provide an overview and analysis of key environment/development issues, and differentiate between negotiable and less negotiable issues.

Strategies can help to overcome problems of organizational and policy fragmentation and compartmentalization by:

- developing multi-agency networks;
- setting in motion analysis of the main constraints to more integrated management;
- providing on-the-job training in integrated management; and
- developing institutions and organizational arrangements that are better equipped to cope with uncertainty, rapid change, and the need for more integrated decisions.

A major obstacle to economic and social development is the shortage of national management skills. Strategies can help to develop these skills. This is especially true of skills in integration: in short supply in both upper-income and lower-income countries.

Strategies, if they are participatory, are likely to be unconstrained by the limits of governance. They will be able to engage both governments and other major actors, such as businesses, communities, and NGOs.

Strategies combine the coherence of plans and the flexibility and opportunism of ad hoc approaches. They can integrate planning with other components of the decision-making system such as investment procedures and political processes.

Box 5: Some benefits of strategies

The following is a sample of the benefits gained so far from a selection of national and provincial strategies. Only a few highlights have been given: not all the benefits from the strategies concerned are included.

Bangladesh (National Conservation Strategy): Better treatment of environmental issues in the Forest Master Plan and the World Bank Third Forestry Project.

Botswana (National Conservation Strategy): Establishment of a National Conservation Strategy Advisory Board and Coordination Agency. Introduction of an environmental impact assessment procedure as part of the national planning and development control system. This has resulted in cost savings from the selection of dam sites, and a reversal of a decision to implement the Southern Okavango Integrated Water Development Project.

Canada (Green Plan): 80 initiatives and programmes on toxic substances, waste reduction, sustainable agriculture, national parks, new technologies for energy efficiency, reduction of ozone depletion, and enforcement of environmental regulations, among others. Legislation on trade in wild animals and plants, and environmental assessment.

Costa Rica (National Conservation Strategy for Sustainable Development): Establishment of the innovative National Biodiversity Institute (INBio). Formation of a National Commission and Master Plan for Environmental Education.

France (National Environmental Action Plan): This crystallized public policy on the environment; set priorities on major environmental issues, to which most interests agreed; helped develop governmental expertise; and led to greater governmental investment in such expertise.

Madagascar (National Environmental Action Plan): Establishment of the Office National de l'Environnement (ONE), a coordinating body within the Ministry of Economy and Planning. Adoption of a comprehensive national policy on the environment. Establishment of two umbrella bodies for environmental NGOs to help local NGOs improve their management capacity.

Malaysia (National Conservation Strategy): Adoption of natural resource accounting and of an environmental auditing system within government. Establishment of a Resources and Environment Section within the Economic Planning Unit.

box continues

Nepal (National Conservation Strategy): Establishment of an environmental core group, an inter-sectoral network consisting of some 70 senior government officials from 20 ministries and departments as well as divisions of the National Planning Commission, to develop new environmental policies and procedures. This group has acted as a catalyst for environmental assessment activities, the establishment of environment units within key government sectors, and the preparation of environmental assessment guidelines for Nepal.

Netherlands (National Environmental Policy Plan): Some major agreements on structural changes in production and consumption have been made. Partnerships of government agencies, industry, business and citizens have been established. There have been 17 covenants signed between governments and industrial sectors and six more are being negotiated. Once these are completed, 80 per cent of the pollution caused by industry in the Netherlands will be covered by covenants to reduce it.

Nicaragua (National Conservation Strategy): Involvement of all of Nicaragua's 143 municipalities in participatory diagnoses of the needs, problems and solutions. This contributed to the national dialogue between antagonists in the recent civil war and launched locally-driven efforts to solve local problems in many parts of the country.

Norway: Annual budgets now contain estimates of environmental effects of the proposed expenditure of each ministry. New environmental planning guidelines have been tested at the local level. EIA rules are being better implemented.

Pakistan (National Conservation Strategy): Effective communication of sustainable development issues and the NCS through the work of the Journalists Resource Centre for the Environment (JRC), established as part of the strategy process. With the recent addition of informal communications programmes such as television, radio, street theatre and participatory methods of communication, the messages of the NCS are reaching many levels of society.

Zambia (National Conservation Strategy): As a result of deliberate and patient capacity-building within mid-level personnel during the development of the NCS, a committed and knowledgeable core of people has been built up within the government to implement the strategy. The group provides an effective base for new institutions, such as the National Environment Council, and a means of internalizing the strategy within government.

Zimbabwe: Greater public awareness of environmental issues.

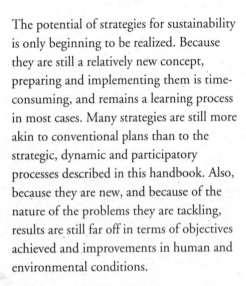

The benefits of strategies to date, including better organization, legislation and procedures, have been significant (see Box 5).

The difficulties with strategies

The potential of strategies for sustainability is only beginning to be realized. Because they are still a relatively new concept, preparing and implementing them is time-consuming, and remains a learning process in most cases. Many strategies are still more akin to conventional plans than to the strategic, dynamic and participatory processes described in this handbook. Also, because they are new, and because of the nature of the problems they are tackling, results are still far off in terms of objectives achieved and improvements in human and environmental conditions.

A strategy is not a panacea. The obstacles to sustainable development discussed earlier can disrupt and impede a strategy and bring it to a halt. It is an ambitious undertaking no matter how well-equipped a country is. Potential problems include the following:

- The concepts of sustainable development and integrating human and ecological concerns are still unfamiliar and poorly worked out. Some of the required methods are not widely known (a constraint that this handbook aims to address). Some remain to be developed and tested.

- The changes promoted by the strategy may include changes in decision-making structures and resource allocation, which may be resisted by those in government and positions of influence.
- The process calls for wide participation and consensus-building, and hence for freedom of expression and assembly, which may not be acceptable to certain forms of government. In addition, consensus is often not possible on issues about which there are deep differences in values.
- Because it deals with complex issues and involves many interest groups, a strategy usually requires time to develop, plus significant managerial and other resources.
- The long-term nature of strategies – optimally longer than the tenure of a particular government – means that their continuity is often at risk.
- The process relies on cross-sectoral thinking and techniques, for which traditions and skills may be weak.
- The process is necessarily experimental: not all outcomes can be foreseen and few can be guaranteed.
- For some issues, external forces beyond the reach of the strategy (like terms of trade and international markets) may be immovable constraints.

Some of these difficulties may prevent the successful development of a strategy. The cyclical nature of strategies allows them to be incremental and flexible. Consequently, many difficulties can be tackled as part of the strategy process. Opportunities for doing this are identified in later chapters. The conditions necessary for an effective national strategy are identified in Chapter 4.

Conclusion

Sustainable development means improving and maintaining the well-being of people and ecosystems. Since we cannot stand still, the alternative to sustainable development is a situation in which ecosystems degrade and lose their viability and people's choices are limited by a mounting struggle against want, insecurity and catastrophe. The poor already live with this situation and there is evidence that it is spreading.

In general, present values, knowledge systems, technologies and institutions make it easier to live unsustainably than sustainably. Changing them is an enormous challenge,

made all the more difficult by the fact that many people feel threatened by change, and viable alternatives are not clear.

An integrated approach to these problems is necessary; one that combines concern for people and concern for ecosystems. Also needed are processes to encourage and focus public discussion, negotiation, mediation, and development of a political consensus. Strategies for sustainability can provide both these needs.

Strategic initiatives like national conservation strategies, environmental actions plans and national development plans provide building blocks and experience for the development of national sustainable development strategies. They show some of the benefits and many of the difficulties of undertaking strategies. Their lessons provide ample material with which to design and undertake an effective strategy for the transition to sustainability.

Endnote

Chapters of Agenda 21 *that describe the need for national strategies: Preamble 1.3; Social and Economic Dimensions 2.6; Combating Poverty 3.9; Changing Consumption Patterns 4.26; Demographic Dynamics and Sustainability 5.31, 5.56; Protection and Promotion of Human Health 6.40; Promoting Sustainable Human Settlement Patterns 7.30, 7.51; Integrating Environment and Development in Decision-Making 8.3, 8.4, 8.7; Protection of the Atmosphere 9.12; Integrated Approach to the Planning and Management of Land Resources 10.6; Combatting Deforestation 11.4, 11.13; Fragile Ecosystems, Desertification and Drought 12.4, 12.37; Sustainable Agriculture 14.4, 14.45; Biodiversity, objectives (b); Biotechnology 16.17; Oceans 17.6, 17.39; Freshwater and Water Resources 18.11, 18.12, 18.40; Toxic Chemicals 19.58; Solid Wastes 21.10, 21.18, 21.30; Local Authorities 23.2; Financial Resources 33.8, 33.22, 33.15; Science 35.7, 35.16; Education 36.5; National Capacity Building 37.4, 37.5, 37.7, 37.10; International Institutions 38.13, 38.25, 38.36, 38.38, 38.39, 38.40; Information 40.4; Rio Declaration – Principle 10; Convention on Biodiversity – Article 6; Convention on Climate Change – Article 3, 4, 12.*

Chapters of Caring for the Earth *that describe the need for national strategies:*

Chapter 8, Providing a National Framework for Integrating Development and Conservation: Action 8.2; Chapter 13, Farm and Range Lands: Action 13.1; Chapter 17, Implementing the Strategy: Action 17.7; Box 31 (Targets – page 180: Adoption by all countries of a national strategy for sustainability by the year 2000); and Annex 8, Strategies for Sustainability.

Chapter 4

Building a National Sustainable Development Strategy

Strategies may be international, national, or local, and they may be sectoral or multi-sectoral. This handbook covers national multi-sectoral strategies. In many countries, economic and environmental strategies are unintegrated, each being undertaken parallel to the other. The number of partially integrated strategies is growing as environment strategies address economic and social concerns, and development plans pay more attention to environmental factors. Although integration is increasing, no fully integrated sustainable development strategy yet exists.

A national sustainable development strategy should build on existing strategy initiatives such as a national conservation strategy, environmental action plan or development plan, or a sectoral or subnational strategy. Only in exceptional circumstances will it need to start from scratch.

Conditions required before developing a multi-sectoral national strategy include: a defined need and purpose; a location for the strategy's steering committee and secretariat where they can have the greatest influence on the national development system; high level support; the commitment of key participants; and a conducive political and social climate.

Necessary conditions that can be generated during the strategy process include: wide understanding of the concepts of sustainable development and the strategy, and of the need for both; clear goals and objectives; a body of well trained, experienced and committed people to drive the strategy; adequate resources; and effective communications.

Many of these conditions can be developed by working on a strategy which is less ambitious than an NSDS, such as a sectoral, regional or local strategy. The feasibility and scope of an NSDS can be determined by assessing whether the conditions can be met (and how to meet them), where change is most needed, how the strategy would relate to the decision-making system, how existing strategy processes can best be enhanced, what resources would be needed, and how they could be provided.

The main kinds of national strategy

The many different kinds of environment and development strategies may be grouped into six categories, depending on their geographical scope – international, national, or local – and on whether they are devoted to a particular sector or theme or are multi-sectoral (Table 1).

- International strategies may be global in scope or cover two or more countries grouped politically or by natural region.
- National strategies focus on a single nation. Various forms of them are described in Box 6. In countries with federal systems, provincial, state or territorial strategies are similar in scope and organization to national strategies.
- Local or regional strategies cover parts of nations or provinces, the parts being defined politically or administratively (municipalities, counties, regional districts, etc) or naturally (coastal zones, drainage basins, mountain ranges, forests, etc).

At present, most multi-sectoral national strategies have a primary focus on either environment or development. Conservation strategies and environmental action plans cover many environmental and resource management issues, from biodiversity to human settlements. They aim to achieve specific conservation or environmental objectives and to integrate environmental conservation into development.

Conservation strategies and environmental action plans point out the contribution of conservation to development, but seldom deal directly with other aspects of development. They tend to have had their strongest inputs from environmental and natural resource interests, and their inclusion of economic and social interests is usually weaker, employing few techniques for examining economic and social issues.

Development plans cover resource allocation, infrastructure development, public investment, employment generation, and many other aspects of economic development. Economic development tends to be interpreted narrowly, however, and environmental and social concerns are rarely treated in depth. Some development plans explicitly recognize the impact of the plan on the environment and the contribution of environmental resources to the plan's objectives. But environmental analysis is usually cursory and poorly integrated with economic analysis.

In many countries, economic and environmental strategies are not integrated. Each is undertaken independently, often at a different time, or, at best, in parallel to the other. Development planning and decision-making largely ignore environmental concerns, including the environmental strategy, if one

Table 1: Classification of selected environment and development strategies

	Multi-sectoral	Sectoral or Thematic
International	• Stockholm Conference Action Plan[1] • World Conservation Strategy[2] • Report of World Commission on Environment and Development (Our Common Future)[3] • Report of Latin American and Caribbean Commission on Development and Environment (Our Own Agenda)[4] • Caring for the Earth: a Strategy for Sustainable Living[5] • Agenda 21[6] • Strategies for shared regions (Regional Seas Programmes, river basin strategies, etc)	• Global Biodiversity Strategy[7] • Tropical Forestry Action Programme[8] • Strategy and Agenda for Action for Sustainable Agriculture and Rural Development[9] • Global Strategy for Health for All by the Year 2000[10] • Plan of Action to Combat Desertification[11] • World Population Action Plan[12] • International Environmental • Education Programme[13] • Vancouver Action Plan for Human Settlements[14] • Mar del Plata Action Plan for Water Resources Development[15] • Strategy for the Protection of the Marine Environment[16] • Climate Change Strategy[17]
National *	• National Development Plans • National Conservation Strategies • National Environmental Action Plans • Green Plans • National Environmental Management Plans • National Sustainable Development Strategies • Provincial conservation and sustainable development strategies	• Sectoral master plans • Tropical Forestry Action Plans • National Plans to Combat Desertification • National or provincial strategies and action plans on biodiversity, climate change, energy, environmental education, indigenous peoples, population, etc.
Regional or local	• Conservation/environmental/ sustainable development strategies and action plans for political/ administrative regions, natural regions, municipalities, etc.	• Regional or local strategies and action plans on biodiversity, climate change, energy, environmental education, indigenous peoples, population, etc.

*Note: shading indicates strategies covered by this book. * National includes provincial or equivalent strategies in countries with a federal system. 1. UN 1972; 2 IUCN/UNEP/WWF 1980; 3. WCED 1987; 4. UNDP/IADB 1990; 5. IUCN/UNEP/WWF 1991; 6. UNCED 1992 7. WRI/UNDP/UNEP 1992; 8. FAO/WRI/W.BANK/ UNDP 1987; 9. FAO 1991; 10. WHO 1981; 11. UNCOD 1977; 12. WPC 1974; 13. UNEP/UNESCO 1975; 14. UNCHS 1976; 15. UNWC 1977; 16. IMO 1983; 17. WMO/UNEP 1992.*

Box 6: *Various types of national strategy*

Many different strategic approaches have been advocated by governments and international agencies in different contexts. They cover a spectrum, from those that focus mainly on environmental concerns and their integration into the development process — for example, the early National Conservation Strategies (NCSs) — to those that deal with social and economic issues as well; for example, later NCSs and National Environmental Action Plans (NEAPs). Of the approaches listed here, NCSs and NEAPs have provided most of the lessons for all forms of strategy development. Both approaches have had their problems and difficulties as well as successes; but, over time, the lessons learned have led to improvements, with some convergence in approach. National strategies fall into two categories: multi-sectoral; and sectoral or thematic.

Multi-sectoral strategies

National Development Plans encompass a wide variety of planning exercises undertaken by national governments, often by the central Ministry of Finance or Development Planning. They are usually for specific periods, and include five-year rolling plans (focusing on increasing productivity or competitiveness, fiscal targets, major infrastructural development, etc); annual budgets; and plans covering human resources, the structure of manufacturing and industry, and public sector enterprises (including investment and privatization). They also include structural adjustment plans negotiated between governments and the International Monetary Fund/World Bank.

National Conservation Strategies were conceived by IUCN, WWF and UNEP (1980 onwards). These were proposed by the World Conservation Strategy (IUCN/WWF/UNDP 1980) as the means of providing a comprehensive, cross-sectoral analysis of conservation and resource management issues, to integrate environmental concerns into the development process. They have aimed to identify the country's most urgent environmental needs, stimulate national debate and raise public consciousness, help decision-makers set priorities and allocate human and financial resources, and build institutional capacity to handle complex environmental issues. NCSs have been strongly process-oriented. Information has been obtained, and analysis undertaken, by cross-sectoral groups. NCSs have sought to develop political consensus around issues identified through such group interaction. Their results include policy documents approved at high level, action plans, and specific programmes and projects.

box continues

National Environmental Action Plans are promoted by the World Bank (1987 onwards) as a condition for receiving loans. These have been undertaken primarily by host country organizations (usually a coordinating ministry) with technical and financial assistance from the World Bank, various international organizations, NGOs and other donors. They have been designed expressly to provide a framework for integrating environmental considerations into a nation's overall economic and social development programs, sometimes in response to structural adjustment imperatives. They also make recommendations for specific actions, outlining the environmental policies, legislation, institutional arrangements, and investment strategies required. They have usually culminated in a package of environmentally-related investment projects, many of which are intended for donor assistance (World Bank 1990, 1991).

Green Plans, produced to date by Canada and the Netherlands, are an evolving process of comprehensive, national programmes for environmental improvement and resource stewardship, with government-wide objectives and commitments. Key goals include cleaner air, water and soil; protection of ecosystems and species; and contributions to global environmental security. The Netherlands National Environmental Policy Plan is radical. It calls for massive reductions in many emissions and wastes within a generation, backed by major clean-up of contaminated sites, to restore and maintain environmental carrying capacity. Targets and schedules provide a means of gauging success and reinforcing the commitment to environmentally responsible decision-making.

National Environmental Management Plans are currently being developed by many island countries of the South Pacific, coordinated by the South Pacific Regional Environment Programme (SPREP) with support from the Asian Development Bank, UNDP and IUCN. These plans follow a process of round table discussions and consultation with key decision-makers and organizations. They lead to the definition of a policy framework and portfolio of programmes and projects for donor support.

National Sustainable Development Strategies (NSDSs) were called for by Caring for the Earth and Agenda 21. In this handbook, we suggest NSDS as a generic name for a participatory and cyclical process of planning and action to achieve economic, ecological and social objectives in a balanced and integrated manner. NSDSs may take many forms, and incorporate or build on many of the above approaches (EAPs, NCSs, etc.).

box continues

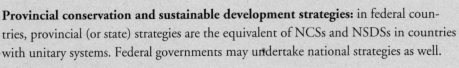

Provincial conservation and sustainable development strategies: in federal countries, provincial (or state) strategies are the equivalent of NCSs and NSDSs in countries with unitary systems. Federal governments may undertake national strategies as well.

Sectoral or thematic strategies

Sectoral Master Plans, such as agricultural sector plans and protected area systems plans, are often prepared as a sectoral expression of a five-year development plan, and as a means to coordinate donor involvement in a sector. They have been widely prepared in Asia, sponsored by the Asian Development Bank, for such sectors as forestry, agriculture and tourism. Most are not participatory processes. Several have involved a massive research and policy development effort over many years, and have attempted to address inter-sectoral issues. The plans are a comprehensive information resource, but some bear little relation to the capacity of the sector to implement them.

Tropical Forestry Action Plans (1986 onwards) are sponsored by FAO and promoted under the Tropical Forestry Action Programme (TFAP). These are related to a global strategy developed by FAO, UNDP, the World Bank and World Resources Institute (FAO/WRI/WB/UNDP 1987). National TFAP exercises are undertaken by the country concerned, starting with a multi-sectoral review of forest-related issues, and leading to policy and strategy plans. They are followed by an implementation phase for policies, programmes and projects. The plan seeks to produce informed decisions and action programmes with explicit national targets on policies and practices, afforestation and forest management, forest conservation and restoration, and integration with other sectors. Round tables involving governmental bodies, NGOs, bilateral and multilateral donor agencies, and international organizations are held at different stages of planning and implementation.

National Plans to Combat Desertification (1985–1988) are sponsored by CILSS (the Permanent Committee for Drought Control in the Sahel). These documents analyze the socio-economic and ecological situation, review current activities and discuss policies and actions required to combat drought; they represent the national anti-desertification plans for a number of Sahelian countries.

In addition, national plans are arising out of the international Climate Change Convention and the Biodiversity Convention, and country poverty assessments are planned by the World Bank.

box continues

Documents contributing to the strategy processes

Various country environmental profiles and state-of-the-environment reports are prepared by governments, bilateral aid donors and NGOs. In general, they present information on conditions and trends, identify and analyze causes, links and constraints, and indicate emerging issues and problems.

UNCED National Reports (1991–1992) on environment and sustainable development are descriptive and analytical documents. They were prepared by national governments, sometimes with NGO involvement. In practice, they varied enormously, but the UNCED Secretariat guidelines proposed that each report should address development trends and environmental impacts and responses to environment and development issues such as principles and goals, policies, legislation, institutions, programmes and projects, and international cooperation. Many countries consulted local, regional and international NGOs and industry. The reports identify how national economic and other activities can stay within the constraints imposed by the need to conserve natural resources. Some consider issues of equity and justice. Certain of them are intended as the foundation for future NSDSs.

CSD National Reports are designed for reporting to the Commission for Sustainable Development on progress in implementing Agenda 21. Few have been produced to date.

Note: The 1993 Directory of Country Environmental Studies (WRI/IIED/IUCN 1992) lists, and provides abstracts for, most of the main documents resulting from the above approaches.

exists. Environmental strategies have been undertaken without sufficient regard for existing planning and decision-making procedures. Some strategies have either duplicated or otherwise failed to coordinate with existing individual sector development plans (such as forestry, agriculture and wildlife). There has often been scant assessment of how the strategy would relate to the development planning system, how to use its strengths, and how to influence it

most effectively. One reason for this is the failure to overcome perceptions of the conservation strategy as anti-development or as applying to only a few sectors.

As environmental strategies address economic and social objectives more directly, and development plans pay more attention to environmental objectives, the number of partially integrated strategies is increasing. They include development plans that have not just an environmental chapter, but incorporate environmental considerations in all chapters. They also include conservation strategies and environmental plans that relate directly to the development planning system, and so have begun to make improvements to the development planning process and sectoral decisions.

There are many reasons for this move towards integration:

- increasing knowledge about development and environment issues and their interactions;
- the emergence of global environmental and development concerns as key international issues;
- greater public interest and pressure for change; and
- the need to define more precise actions, including an environmental investment portfolio.

We know of no example of a fully integrated strategy; one that combines all aspects of social, economic and environmental policy into a sustainable development strategy, as called for by Agenda 21 and Caring for the Earth. The trend is clearly in this direction, however. Sustainable development strategies have the potential to replace the development planning process as we know it today.

The history of national strategies

Placing national strategies for sustainable development in a historical context can help to ease the confusion felt by governments and communities when confronted with the vast array of unrelated strategy options, models and demands on their limited resources.

The momentum for national strategies has built up over the past 30 years. The various approaches have evolved in three broad stages, leading gradually to greater emphasis on local initiative.

- For some ten years from the early 1970s, effort was concentrated on developing international strategies to tackle specific problems such as population, human settlements and pollution.
- The 1980s saw the international effort overlaid by a growing interest in more comprehensive strategies at a national level among governments of both north and south. By the end of 1994, more than 100 countries will have embarked upon some form of comprehensive national strategy process; all striving for cross-sectoral relevance and impact.
- The 1990s have seen an emphasis placed on the need to build capacities to institutionalize and refine these processes with growing attention to the sub-national or local level, for that is where action takes effect. Each level continues to be important in building the global strategic framework for sustainable development.

International efforts to nurture cooperative management of common resources have been limited by the ability of each participating country to act. Governments have accepted a growing range of international obligations and have needed to express these in umbrella national strategies.

A recent example is the Convention on Biodiversity Conservation, which calls for the preparation of national biodiversity strategies. Initially, countries took their lead from the World Conservation Strategy (WCS), published in 1980. The WCS introduced the term 'sustainable development' and promoted the preparation of national conservation strategies (NCSs). This concept, based on a process of consensus-building, was the main guiding force in national attempts to reconcile conservation with development for the first half of the 1980s. By 1985, some 30 countries had embarked on a NCS process, largely in isolation from one another but often with assistance from IUCN, which was learning as it went along.

The World Commission on Environment and Development (WCED), which ran from 1985 to 1987, reinforced the value of national strategic approaches and led to a second wave of initiatives. What was becoming apparent during this period was the need for a new, strategic, inter-sectoral approach to managing change; an approach that would overcome the weaknesses of economic planning and piecemeal environment protection policies.

At that time, a number of international organizations came on the scene, with a variety of thematic strategies for selected countries. This greatly complicated the situation. Until then, strategies generally had been the initiatives of governments or national groups, proceeding at a pace and pattern best suited to them. From 1985 on, in response to a global action plan on drought, the United Nations Sudano-Sahelian Office (UNSO) for Africa supported the preparation of national plans to combat desertification. A year later, after the development of a global forestry strategy, the Food and Agricultural Organization (FAO) began sponsoring the preparation of national Tropical Forestry Action Plans (TFAPs). To date, TFAPs have been prepared for 91 countries in all parts of the world. In 1987, the World Bank began helping four countries in Africa prepare National Environment Action Plans (NEAPs). By 1991, ten additional NEAPs had been started. These were in response to an internal World Bank directive, requiring action plans as a Bank loan precondition for the least developed countries. In 1992, this directive was reinforced and expanded to cover all 110 of the Bank's borrower countries.

It was appropriate that the next major addition to the strategies family should

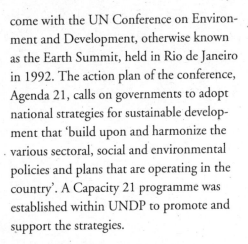

come with the UN Conference on Environment and Development, otherwise known as the Earth Summit, held in Rio de Janeiro in 1992. The action plan of the conference, Agenda 21, calls on governments to adopt national strategies for sustainable development that 'build upon and harmonize the various sectoral, social and environmental policies and plans that are operating in the country'. A Capacity 21 programme was established within UNDP to promote and support the strategies.

The labels in this smorgasbord of strategies – for example, NCSs, TFAPs, NEAPs, NSDSs, Green Plans and NEMPs (National Environment Management Plans in the South Pacific) – imply that each is a distinct entity. In practice, this is not so: there is a great diversity within each type, and overlap among them. Yet one can safely generalize that strategies which have departed from the original model to express true national identity have tended to be the most successful.

Entry points into a multi-sectoral national strategy

It is likely that some kind of strategy on environment and development is being, or has been, undertaken in most countries. Fresh initiatives should be linked to ongoing or past processes, and be clearly identified as extensions or components of them. NSDSs and other multi-sectoral strategies should build on existing strategic initiatives, not attempt to duplicate or ignore them. Some NEAPs, for example, have ignored established NCSs. Substantial investments have already been made in these existing processes. New investment is likely to be more effective if it draws upon and enhances these processes and does not distract, undermine or devalue them.

The object is not to create a new or separate sustainable development process but to improve existing processes of planning and decision-making. National economic plans, and longer-term strategies such as Malaysia's *Vision 2020*, are highly influential because they are linked to powerful economic, industrial and financial ministries. NSDSs should be fully integrated with these plans. Otherwise they risk being marginalized as outside the mainstream of national priorities, and they may be unable to influence the main economic agents of change.

Entry into the kind of multi-sectoral strategy cycle described in this handbook will therefore probably involve one of the following:

- the further development of an existing multi-sectoral national strategy, such as a National Development Plan, National Conservation Strategy, or Environmental Action Plan;
- expanding a narrowly-focused initiative, such as a structural adjustment programme;

- building on a sectoral or thematic strategy or on a multi-sectoral regional or local strategy; and
- start-up (although this implies starting from scratch, all countries have some form of policy-making and planning process on which to build).

Necessary conditions

The conditions required for an effective multi-sectoral national strategy depend on its scope. The more comprehensive a strategy, the more complex it is. It will require a bigger information base and a wider range of participants. It also demands more money and professional staff with considerably more integration and management skills.

Many difficulties with national strategies have been due to inexperience and lack of appropriate models. Sometimes problems have been severe enough to cause the strategies to lose momentum, reach an impasse on critical issues, lose leadership and vision, or even be abandoned. In some cases, countries have embarked on multi-sectoral strategies before they were ready for them. The necessary conditions and capacity may need to be developed gradually, through a less ambitious strategy process that, in due course, can be made more comprehensive.

Conditions before developing the strategy

Necessary conditions required before developing a multi-sectoral national strategy include:

1. A defined need and purpose. The need for a strategy, as the best response to well identified problems, must be evident. It may be that a multi-sectoral national strategy is not an appropriate course of action. A thematic strategy, local strategy, or some more specific action may be better for the time being.

2. A location for the steering committee and secretariat where they can have the greatest influence on the national development system. It is impossible to develop and implement a strategy without a clear decision about which organization is directly responsible for it. If the strategy is to be influential, the organization has to be influential.

3. High level support. Political support at a high level – parliamentary, cabinet or head of state – is crucial for the development of a strategy. Support must be visible, and must be based on an understanding of the strategy process and its costs and likely benefits. Since the strategy includes the formulation and implementation of government policy, the highest levels must both support the strategy process and understand its products as they evolve. This support should include:

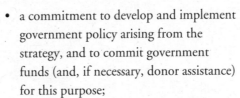

- a commitment to develop and implement government policy arising from the strategy, and to commit government funds (and, if necessary, donor assistance) for this purpose;
- the intention to follow and to consider the policy implications of the strategy throughout the process, and not merely to consider the whole strategy agenda whenever it is formally submitted for adoption;
- instructions to government departments that their policy formulation and planning should be coordinated with the strategy, unless the topic is outside the scope of the strategy; and
- the intention to keep the strategy process open and inclusive, and not confidential and closed – encouraging participation in the strategy, giving participants ready access to information, and encouraging them to adopt critical approaches.

4. The commitment of key participants. The participation of certain groups and individuals will depend on the strategy's scope and purpose. Obviously their participation is essential; if some cannot be induced to participate, this is a sign of inadequate support. A more limited strategy, requiring the involvement of only those who are keen to participate, should be considered, with a view to bringing others on board as the strategy gains in momentum and support.

5. A conducive political and social climate. Political unrest will make it difficult, if not impossible, to develop a strategy, mainly because the necessary broad consensus cannot be reached. However, the situation shortly after a major political change could provide the right stimulus. Political conditions must be conducive to free speech and participation, giving confidence for creative thinking and a mandate to think critically.

Conditions that should be provided while developing the strategy

Necessary conditions that can be generated while developing a strategy include:

1. Wide understanding within the country of the concepts of sustainable development and the strategy; and of the need for both. This can be developed in the course of the strategy, provided a nucleus of key people and organizations are supportive from the outset.

2. Clear objectives, together with a monitoring mechanism, so that the strategy continues to pursue them and is not diverted or hijacked. The objectives have to be those of the people implementing the strategy, and so must be set in a participatory manner. They can be refined as the strategy progresses.

3. An engine to drive the strategy, including well-trained and experienced personnel. A body of committed people inside and outside government is needed to drive the strategy throughout, and to provide the main energy source. Capable staff with good management skills and judgement are essential for managing the strategy process. The capacity to manage the process can be developed as part of the strategy.

4. Adequate resources. Funds have to be available, either from national sources or a combination of national sources and donor funding (see Chapter 10 on donor support). National sources include special allocations of government revenue, adjustments to existing government sectoral budgets and investment plans, the corporate sector, and other participants, such as NGOs. The minimum required is for a steering committee and secretariat to carry out core functions of policy review and development and initial capacity-building activities.

5. Effective communication. Communication is the means by which participants in the strategy:

- exchange information with each other;
- reach agreement with each other on actions;
- undertake actions to change or strengthen values and knowledge; and
- inform others about the strategy.

Together with participation, communication is the crucial element of the strategy, pervading all others. A communications plan needs to be developed and implemented, covering modes and frequency of communication among participants and between participants and others.

Overcoming obstacles

Several obstacles must be overcome in order to foster the conditions for an effective strategy.

Lack of support

A lack of high-level support for a strategy can be overcome by developing awareness and support among interest groups and the public, and by taking every advantage of events that publicize the need for and benefits of a strategy. Many strategies received their initial stimulus from international initiatives, notably the World Conservation Strategy, the report of the WCED (Our Common Future), and UNCED's Agenda 21. Others have been galvanized by disasters and crises such as the Mount Pinatubo eruption in the Philippines. In Zimbabwe, politicians were influenced to support the development of the national conservation strategy when they were flown to a drought-stricken region and saw for themselves the full extent of land degradation.

Lack of capacity

If there is a lack of well-trained personnel, experience or resources, there are several ways to build on, and learn by, experience, using limited resources. One way is to form a team to undertake projects that could eventually contribute to a strategy. Bhutan, for example, has begun by forming a National Environmental Secretariat, with close working ties to the National Planning Commission, whose first task has been to develop an environmental assessment procedure for the country.

Another option is to develop either a thematic or a local strategy first. The more modest subject scope of a thematic strategy (covering a single theme such as energy or forestry), and the geographical scope of a local strategy (covering a region or locality), can make them suitable as pilot projects. Through them, the necessary skills can be developed in strategy preparation and implementation, including integrating sectors and managing a complex participatory process. Guinea-Bissau is an example of a small, yet highly diverse country that is developing four local strategies and a regional strategy to gain experience and build the capacity to undertake a national strategy. An advantage of these local strategies is that they cover areas that, ethnically, economically and ecologically, are relatively homogeneous. This makes it easier to find solutions toward sustainable development, although difficulties remain in obtaining the support of national authorities for local development plans. The regional strategy covers half the area of the country and two-thirds of its population. So its problems are similar to those that would be faced by a national strategy, but on a somewhat more manageable scale.

Determining the scope

National, local, or sectoral strategies: which comes first?

The variety of national approaches suggests that every answer is potentially correct. Malaysia began with state conservation strategies before embarking on a national conservation strategy, while Pakistan and Zambia developed their national conservation strategy first, and are now developing provincial conservation strategies. Australia's national conservation strategy led to Victoria's state conservation strategy, which, in turn, provided a framework for municipal conservation strategies. Several of Canada's provinces and territories undertook strategies before the federal government; and in some provinces, the first strategies were at the local level. In Cuba, regional multi-sectoral strategies provided crucial experience for the development of a national sectoral strategy (on protected areas). Guatemala has also started regionally (in Petén). Nicaragua began at the national level, but involved all municipalities in developing the strategy. Ethiopia's national strategy is being

Box 7: Many strategies but no strategy? The case of British Columbia

The Canadian province of British Columbia illustrates the complex mixture of strategies that can arise as governments respond to different political pressures. The province has several thematic strategies (such as biodiversity and protected areas); two multi-sectoral strategies (the Strategy for Sustainability and the Land Use Strategy) and a number of local strategies. Connections among the strategies are not entirely clear.

The Strategy for Sustainability is being developed by an advisory body: the Round Table on the Environment and the Economy. It focuses on selected issues: energy, an economic framework, education, and community sustainability.

The Land Use Strategy is being developed by all groups with an interest in land use (a great many), guided by an independent statutory body: the Commission on Resources and Environment. The strategy is conceived as having three levels: provincial (a framework for the entire province); regional (involving negotiation and allocation of land among the main types of uses); and local (involving detailed management by users, communities and government agencies). Logically, the provincial framework would have been developed first. But allocation of land in regions such as Vancouver Island is politically much more pressing. Consequently, although the strategy is expected eventually to have local and provincial levels, the regional level is being worked on first.

Several local strategies have been developed, mostly in areas where land use controversies are particularly heated. Many were initiated before the land use strategy began.

In short, British Columbia has sectoral and multi-sectoral strategies at local, regional and provincial levels. The scope and level of the strategies has been determined in response to the political needs of the day. This has given each strategy a high degree of political support, at least initially. Also, the number of different strategies at different levels has provided opportunities for a great many different interest groups, agencies and individuals to be involved in the debate on, and movement toward, sustainable development. They have also gained valuable experience in undertaking strategies.

However, the somewhat confusing and ad hoc array of strategic initiatives, coupled with poorly developed links with other decision-making machinery, has its costs.

elaborated through a set of regional processes. The province of British Columbia has multi-sectoral, sectoral and local strategies (Box 7).

Local or regional multi-sectoral strategies and national thematic strategies are valuable for developing experience and building capacities to undertake more complex national strategies. But they are not without problems and are only effective where supported by a suitable national policy framework. Local resource allocation and management decisions taken without reference to national priorities and criteria can result in unacceptable disparities with other areas or simply may be impossible to implement. The success of the Tortuguero Conservation Strategy, a local strategy to control the expansion of banana plantations in Costa Rica, depends not only on actions it is generating at the community level but also on national-level actions.

Local strategies often consist of a mixture of actions undertaken by the participants and recommended actions to be undertaken by higher-level government authorities. Appropriate national policies can define the scope of such recommendations and so ensure that the expectations of the local strategy are realistic. A local strategy in Canada collapsed because of the lack of policies at the provincial level that would have enabled strategy participants to strike an acceptable balance between jobs and protected areas.

There are also risks to undertaking a thematic or sectoral strategy before a multi-sectoral strategy. Sectoral strategies often ignore important inter-sectoral links and impacts. It may prove difficult for an eventual multi-sectoral strategy to harmonize different thematic or sectoral strategies that have been developed in isolation.

Ideally, a national multi-sectoral strategy should be developed before local or sectoral strategies, because it can provide a framework for all other strategies whereas local and sectoral strategies cannot. But if it is easier or more effective to develop a local or sectoral strategy first – or if one or the other is necessary to build capacity or support for a national multi-sectoral strategy – then the local or sectoral strategy should come first.

These are key questions that will help to determine whether to undertake a national multi-sectoral strategy, a national sectoral strategy, or a regional or local strategy:

- Where is the need for change most critical: the nation, a region, a local area, or a sector? Would policies at a higher (eg national) level constrain or foster the possibilities for change at a lower (eg local) level?
- What organizational/staffing/financial capacity is required for the strategy?
- What conditions for an effective strategy are missing and how could they be fostered?
- What can be done with minimal external assistance?

The decision-making system and existing strategies

Where does the NSDS fit in the decision-making system and how does it relate to existing initiatives? In practice, almost all countries are already likely to have several multi-sectoral and sectoral strategies or strategy-like initiatives at national, local and intermediate levels. The questions then are:

- How would the national sustainable development strategy relate to existing planning and decision-making processes? Does it fill a clear niche?
- What opportunities are there to build on and enhance existing strategy processes and structures? Should the national sustainable development strategy: a) be developed from an existing strategy? If so, which one?; b) start off as a coordinating framework for several existing initiatives, and be developed from there? If so, which strategies and related initiatives most need coordination?; or c) be developed from scratch?

The desirable alternatives are a) or b). Alternative c) would apply only in the unlikely situation of a complete absence of strategic initiatives; if there had been a long gap since the last initiative ceased to play any meaningful role in the country; or if there were unacceptable political costs associated with existing or recent initiatives.

Upgrading an existing strategy

There are several ways of developing one or more existing strategies into a National Sustainable Development Strategy.

If there is an economic development plan but no conservation strategy or environmental action plan, then the latter could be prepared, although there is a risk that it would be a poor relation of the development plan. To avoid this:

- the agencies and planning team responsible for the development plan should be closely involved in the conservation strategy; and
- the development plan and conservation strategy should be closely linked, with the scope and content of the two corresponding to each other – one providing the socio-economic perspective, the other the socio-environmental perspective (obviously this will entail modifying the development plan, including expanding its scope).

An alternative procedure would be review, modify and expand the development plan so that it provided fully for conservation of ecological processes and biodiversity, protection of natural and cultural heritage, and sustainable use of resources.

Similarly, if a conservation strategy or environmental action plan exists but there is no economic development plan (often the case in upper-income countries), then the conservation strategy could be reviewed, modified and expanded to address social and economic objectives.

In either case, the logical time for modification and expansion is when the development plan or conservation strategy is due for review. Expanding the scope will involve widening the range of participants in the strategy. Environmental interests and sectors would participate in the development plan; and development sectors and interests would participate in the conservation strategy.

Modifications to the existing development plan or conservation strategy might include:

- Incorporating environmental factors in economic policies, plans and decisions.
- Developing institutions to integrate social, economic, and environmental objectives.
- Incorporating environmental components throughout the development plan. Each sector would identify the contribution of environmental goods and services to the sector and the sector's impact on the environment. The plan would include policies and measures to maintain the environmental goods and services and reduce impacts on the environment. Priority would be given to those areas where environmental goods and services are most at risk or environmental impacts are most severe.

- Incorporating socio-economic components throughout the conservation strategy or environmental action plan. The strategy would address not merely how to ensure that economic activities are environ-mentally sound, but how to improve economic performance in ways that are ecologically sustainable and how to improve the quality of life in ways that are economically viable.

The most appropriate course is to combine development and environmental initiatives into one initiative, involving participants in existing multi-sectoral strategies, and building on the processes, institutions, policies and agreements of those strategies.

An NSDS could start out as a simple way to coordinate and provide a framework for the often-large number of development and environment initiatives that a country pursues at any one time. These may include a national development plan, national conservation strategy, environmental action plan, forestry action plan, biodiversity strategy, and Agenda 21. Without such a framework, there is a risk of conflict and duplication and of new initiatives diverting attention and resources from the overall process.

Chapter 5

Participation in Strategies

Sustainable development involves trade-offs between economic, social and ecological objectives. Such trade-offs cannot be determined by 'scientific' means alone, no matter how multi-disciplinary. They are value judgements, and therefore 'people-centered' approaches to sustainable development strategies are needed. Participation of stakeholder groups is critical for decision-making, and for all tasks of the strategy cycle, taking different forms for each task. The result will be a more realistic strategy, with a broader base of knowledge, understanding and commitment from the groups involved, and with better links to promising local initiatives.

The challenge of participation is considerable: 'horizontal' participation across sectors and geographic regions has to be complemented by 'vertical' participation from national to local levels. Although existing structures and methods for participation are usually weak, it is best to begin by using them. Introducing new elements – participatory inquiry, communications/information and education campaigns, round tables and special committees – is relatively easy and can have great impact. NGOs and local governments can help to bring this about. It is a mistake to think that participation is entirely a non-government affair: ultimately, governments need to find appropriate roles as facilitators in participation, and hence to continually increase the effectiveness of strategies.

Why participation is integral

People involved in strategies for sustainability commonly say that what is important is not the strategy document itself, which becomes outdated almost as soon as it is published, but the strategy's beneficial products in terms of:

- enhanced understanding of sustainable development issues, both within and between interest groups;
- improved communications within and between interest groups;
- consensus on the main issues, and what to do about them;
- networks of committed individuals and institutions; and
- renegotiations of responsibility between interests, and joint actions for sustainable development.

In other words, successful strategies are participatory. Conversely, 'failed' strategies – those that appear to be going nowhere, even though the documentation may look good – are frequently characterized by a lack of participation.

'Tell me and I'll forget; show me and I may remember: involve me and I'll understand.'

quoted by Andrew Campbell, Landcare, Australia

Few strategies, however, have been either entirely participatory or completely non-participatory. Most strategies, to get close to their declared objectives, have had to incorporate existing participation structures and methodologies, improve them or even create new ones.

Agenda 21 echoes these observations. Not only does it call for NSDSs as the principal vehicles for addressing Agenda 21 at national level, but it also recommends that they be developed 'with the widest possible participation'. How can this be done? So far, beyond general observations, there has been little analysis of how participation has taken place in previous strategies, the impacts of this, and the constraints to improvement. There are many challenges; notably, how to focus efforts given the potentially limitless scope of participation and the down-to-earth realities of limited resources and time; and how to build participation into strategies born of bureaucratic or donor initiatives, which themselves are not always conducive to participation.

Sustainable development can be thought of as the balanced achievement of economic, environmental and social goals. This involves the integration of these goals where possible, and making trade-offs among them where necessary. In such a balancing act, however, specific local needs and circumstances must be acknowledged – there is no single mix of goals that is right for every group in every country. Neither is the right mix static: it will evolve over time. A further balancing act is needed to determine the trade-offs between the current generation and the next. Uncertainties in the environmental system (such as climate change), in the economic system (such as commodity price changes) and in the social system (such as changing numbers of people and their values) need to be accommodated.

One might assume that a judicious mix of economic, environmental and social sciences can arrive at the right balance between goals, and between generations. In practice, however, this is shown not to be the case. A 'science-based' approach such as this should be complemented by a more 'people-centred' approach. This is because:

- Economic, environmental and social goals are value-laden. Therefore local values, as well as local knowledge and ideas, need to be integrated with scientific analyses in strategic decisions. Multiple perspectives should be sought.
- Sustainable development requires the joint awareness and action of governments, communities and individuals. The individual is ultimately the key player. Sustainable development will, in practice, be the result of many millions of actors working separately and together.

Clearly a strategy cannot be planned and implemented by government alone. All actors need to be motivated to deliver a sustainable future. In trade-offs, some actors will be 'losers' and others will be 'winners'.

Debate, consensus-building, commitment and action is essential – by both 'winners' and 'losers', and by those who are central to power as well as those who have been marginalized in the past. This is particularly so in the context of a strategy. All parties need to feel some ownership and commitment to the process. A range of groups will be required to act, often jointly, in order for the strategy to be implemented; but each group must feel the actions meet their individual, as well as collective, goals. This is difficult to achieve. A key element is to seek a mandate from affected groups before the strategy policies are defined.

A common response by governments to the challenges of a comprehensive national strategy has been to 'go it alone', often under pressure from development banks. They have viewed the process as a multi-disciplinary, scientific and governmental planning exercise (perhaps involving the academic community). There is a clear distinction between participatory and multi-disiplinary methods, yet these two approaches are not mutually exclusive. Land-use planning and Geographic Information Systems are usually low in participation and higher in multi-disciplinary methods; whereas participatory rural appraisal is very high in participation and not very multi-disciplinary (Carley 1994).

To be effective, national strategies need to be both highly participatory and highly multi-disciplinary. The challenge is to

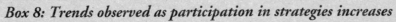

Box 8: *Trends observed as participation in strategies increases*

- NGOs, local governments and other catalysts provide more opportunities for participation.
- More use is made of participatory methodologies to gain information on local situations, views and needs.
- External agents facilitate activities, rather than directing or managing them.
- More tasks are done in a participatory way, especially making decisions.
- Decisions are more usually based around consensus.
- More networks are formed.
- More local groups are formed.
- Local groups are increasingly empowered to be active in strategy development and in implementation.
- These groups exercise more local control of resources.
- More work is done jointly, or repartitioned, between government and locals.
- There is increasing emphasis on learning, and approaches are more adaptive.
- Policies and plans become increasingly coherent across sectors.
- The costs of participation, which are initially high, drop considerably.
- The work takes more time, but has greater impact.
- Work programmes become more feasible and practical.
- The institutional environment becomes receptive to further participation.

accomplish this in an efficient manner, establishing a balance that best reflects society's varied perspectives and needs.

It is helpful to consider participation in strategies as a sharing by groups of people in all the tasks ultimately affecting them (information gathering, analysis, decision-making, implementation and capacity-building, and monitoring and evaluation).

Some approaches to participation, in the process of defining the balance among eco-nomic, social and environmental goals, and between the present and the future, margin-alize affected groups or limit their stake. Box 8 lists trends associated with the progression from activities with lower levels of partici-pation to those with higher participation.

The time taken by participatory work tends to be longer than with normal planning/project cycles, at least in the first year or so. This is because groups need to form and consult with their constituencies, and debate issues and objectives in a more lengthy manner than with strategies prepared by 'professionals' alone.

The benefits of participation

The benefits of participation tend to differ with the different tasks, and iterations, of the strategy cycle. They may be summarized by strategy task, as follows:

Participation in information and analysis brings:

- a broad knowledge base and spread of opinion, offering the best informed judgement on issues, trade-offs and options in the time available;
- increased debate, mutual education, understanding of major issues both within and between different groups; and
- the tackling of issues that cannot be identified, properly defined or dealt with by other means (ie, changing values, local conditions, rights and claims and lifestyles, and particularly issues like poverty which otherwise may be submerged).

Participation in policy formulation and planning creates:

- practical and realistic objectives, targets and standards, which are negotiated so that they are locally acceptable, meaningful and practicable;
- 'ownership' of, and commitment to, the strategy, built up by groups actually working on it (essential if the strategy is

to result in social mobilization);
- greater political credibility of the strategy than were it just a product of technicians and bureaucrats; and
- accountability and transparency – people can see what 'government' does.

Participation in implementation and monitoring achieves:

- increased capacity (learning by exposure and debate; learning by doing);
- more extensive networks for tasks (for example, monitoring);
- increased momentum and coverage in action programmes through expansion of networks and others buying into the process; and
- efficient mobilization and management of resources and skills.

The costs of participation

Generally, the more participants in a strategy, the higher are the costs of participation. These costs are a function of:

Time requirements. The time commitment to participation will depend on the strategy component and the maturity of the strategy process (ie, how many turns of the cycle have been completed). The planning or policy formulation component has taken three to six months for some World Bank NEAPs with minimal participation. Conversely, it has taken from 18 months to four years to set up and undertake the more

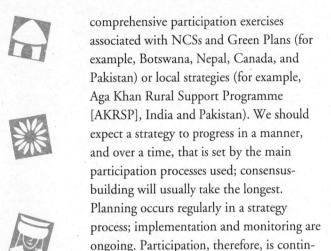

comprehensive participation exercises associated with NCSs and Green Plans (for example, Botswana, Nepal, Canada, and Pakistan) or local strategies (for example, Aga Khan Rural Support Programme [AKRSP], India and Pakistan). We should expect a strategy to progress in a manner, and over a time, that is set by the main participation processes used; consensus-building will usually take the longest. Planning occurs regularly in a strategy process; implementation and monitoring are ongoing. Participation, therefore, is continuous, changing in form, function and breadth throughout the strategy cycle.

Specialist skill requirements. Skills in participatory inquiry, communications, education and media activities are all essential in order to establish the right links and ensure a high quality of communication and participation. Strategies have involved journalists (Nepal), graphic designers and environmental educationalists (Pakistan, Zambia), and participatory rural appraisal staff (AKRSP) to facilitate the communication flow. Each exercise tends to take a specific slant: we do not yet know of a national-level exercise that has consistently employed a broad range of communication skills.

Communications requirements. Participation exercises require the means for different groups to meet at various levels in the field (transport, meeting rooms and equipment), and to communicate through the medium appropriate to the groups in question

(telecommunications, mass media, traditional media, etc). The role of public information, education and communications (IEC) in strategies is considered in the final section of this chapter.

Management requirements of the participation process. The management of all participatory components is complex, and requires professionals with advanced administration skills and those who know how to apply the various skills and methodologies to the appropriate participation structures available in the country. However, process management should not amount to orchestration; there is a need for skilled facilitation. The outcome of participatory activities will be only as socially and politically diverse as the openness of the facilitators permits.

Initial participation exercises in strategies tend to be relatively expensive; the costs of making contact, establishing mechanisms, etc, can be high. Many 'failed' participation exercises are the result of early abandonment (within the first year or two) as patience with the necessarily slow and sometimes experimental start to participation wears thin in the face of donor or governmental pressures for a 'product'.

Experience with participation exercises in major local strategies shows that the costs can go down considerably with each iteration; as the scope, purpose and methodologies for participation of each group in each strategy task become clearer and better focused in the strategy work plan.

The risks of participation

A balance must be struck between involving as wide a range of participants as possible to forge a broad-based and durable consensus without overloading the facilitating and mana-gerial capacities of the animators and leaders of the strategy. The more well-developed and representative the existing participation mechanisms, the more cost-effective they are likely to be. If managerial capacities are weak and participatory mechanisms are poor, the number of participants can be limited at first; but participation should be increased with the development and reiteration of strategy tasks.

The more immediate risks of a participatory approach, as opposed to a top-down approach, are:

- The strategic vision/direction may be less clear, at least for the first year or so. Given the multiple perspectives incorporated, it may be more difficult to focus on priorities.
- Momentum may be lost, as the time taken for participatory strategies is longer. This is possible at both 'higher' levels, including donors, and 'lower' levels; but can be minimized by regular feedback of information (and, most important, by implementing policies on which

consensus has already been reached at the earliest stage possible).
- The integrated approach to social, environmental and economic problems that comes with broad participation is more complex than a single system of analysis and response.
- Control over certain critical aspects (for example, pollution regulation) may be lost if responsibilities become spread too thin among participants.
- If improperly managed, the participatory processes can result in expectations being raised too high among certain groups; more issues being identified than can be dealt with; or impasses and conflicts where consensus or compromise cannot be reached.
- There are political risks of stimulating or aggravating conflicts between groups, or having the process co-opted by elites.

These risks can be minimized through good planning for participation, good management of the participation process and through maintaining independence from party politics. Adequate time, and a determination not to rush into producing a document or into taking precipitous actions, are required.

The use of participatory approaches should not be a one-off event, but be part of a process in which incremental learning is one step in a longer-term commitment to adaptive planning and sustainable development. Success will come only with the

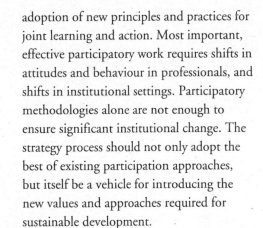

adoption of new principles and practices for joint learning and action. Most important, effective participatory work requires shifts in attitudes and behaviour in professionals, and shifts in institutional settings. Participatory methodologies alone are not enough to ensure significant institutional change. The strategy process should not only adopt the best of existing participation approaches, but itself be a vehicle for introducing the new values and approaches required for sustainable development.

Structures and methods for participation

The strategy should build on the structures and methodologies available for participation in the country or locality.

Examples of existing systems and institutions on which to build include the planning system, the political system, traditional structures (for example, village-based systems) religious systems, the education system, the agricultural extension system, the arts/theatre and the media.

In the absence or weakness of existing participatory structures, informal or one-off structures can be put together specially for the strategy process; for example, special committees and round tables – constituted for the strategy – to discuss specific common or cross-sectoral issues. This is a very common approach, at least for the first iteration of a strategy.

Methodologies which a strategy can utilise include participatory inquiry, resource surveys, 'Green' audits, consensus-building, planning methods, EIA negotiation, voluntary agreements, joint management, traditional methods (for example, of conflict resolution), media techniques (for example, 'phone-ins') and communications and information techniques.

All of these methods need to become well-known and routinely used. Special efforts should be made to build capacity in them even before a strategy begins. Experience in major local strategies has shown that the early development of participatory inquiry has been particularly critical. This explains why there are so many variants of participatory inquiry established under different names for local circumstances (see Box 9).

Consensus

One of the aims of participation is to develop a strategy with a broad base of support. This requires building consensus among participants on objectives, principles, issues, priorities, policies and actions.

In many strategy processes, decisions by the steering committee and other committees are also made by consensus, although consensus is not always clearly defined. Consensus means general agreement: a condition in which all participants can live with the result, although not all (and maybe

Box 9: Participatory inquiry

In recent years, there has been a blossoming of participatory approaches for research, extension, planning and monitoring. Some focus on problem diagnosis; others are more oriented to community empowerment. Some participatory approaches in rural areas concentrate on facilitating on-farm or farmer-led research. Other approaches are designed to get professionals in the field listening to farmers. Some have been developed in the health context; some for watershed management; and some for food security assessment. Some have been developed in government extension institutions and others in NGOs. This diversity of names, applications and 'owners' is a sign of strength. It implies that each variant is to some extent dependent on location-specific contexts and problems.

These new approaches and methods imply downwards shifts of initiative, responsibility and action; especially to farmers and rural people themselves. Earlier investigations, where researchers collected data and took it away for processing, are superseded by more investigation and analysis by local people, who share their knowledge and insights with outsiders. Methods like participatory mapping, analysis of aerial photographs, matrix scoring and ranking, flow and link diagramming, seasonal analysis, and trend diagramming are not just means for farmers to inform outsiders, but methods for farmers' own analysis.

Even though there is great difference between these approaches, a series of common principles underpin most of them:

- A defined methodology and systematic learning process: in each case this focuses on cumulative learning.
- Multiple perspectives: the objective is to seek diversity, rather than characterise complexity in terms of average values.
- Group inquiry process: this implies three types of mix, namely multi-disciplinary; multi-sectoral; and mixes of outsiders (professionals) and insiders (local people).
- Context-specific: the methodology is flexible enough to be adapted and changed to suit each new set of conditions and actors.
- Facilitating experts: the role of the 'expert' is best thought of as helping the people in their situation carry out their own study.
- Leading to action: the inquiry process leads to debate about change, and debate changes the perceptions of the actors and their readiness to contemplate action. Action is agreed, and implementable changes will therefore represent an accommodation between the different conflicting views.

box continues

Participatory inquiry is the methodology that overarches these approaches and their methods. In the strategy process, inquiry occurs during appraisal, planning, implementation, monitoring and evaluation. It is also used in the context of research, extension and education. The techniques of participatory inquiry cover:

- **Group and team dynamics**
  Team contracts
  Team reviews and discussions
  Interview checklists
  Rapid report writing
  Energizers
  Role reversals/work-sharing
  Villager and shared presentations
  Process notes and personal diaries
- **Interviewing and Dialogue**
  Semi-structured interviewing
  Direct observation
  Focus groups
  Key informants
  Ethno-histories and biographies
  Local stories, portraits and case studies

- **Sampling**
  Transect walks
  Wealth ranking and well-being analysis
  Social maps
  Interview maps
- **Visualization and Diagramming**
  Mapping and modelling
  Mobility maps
  Seasonal calendars
  Daily routines, activity profiles
  Historical profiles
  Trend analyses and time lines
  Matrix scoring
  Preference or pairwise ranking
  Venn diagrams
  Network diagrams
  Flow diagrams
  Pie diagrams

Methods which contribute to participatory inquiry include participatory rural appraisal, participatory action research, Diagnostico Rural Rapido, Farmer Participatory Research and Groupe de recherche et d'appui pour l'auto-promotion paysanne.
Source: Pretty (1993).

none) of them may embrace it with great enthusiasm. Consensus does not mean wholehearted agreement or unanimity; differing views, values, and perspectives are a fact of life. Nor does consensus mean

majority agreement, whereby minority concerns are effectively excluded.

When a strategy is implemented by several entities, the policy and plan are negotiated and developed collaboratively by them all. For such a process to work, all participants must have a roughly equal incentive to reach agreement and work together. Consensus then becomes a particularly valuable basis of agreement, because no participant can be outvoted. All participants are obliged to do their best to accommodate each others' interests – or to compromise – to reach agreement where possible, and to identify remaining contentious issues to be resolved later.

Either the mandating authority or the steering committee should produce guidelines on what to do when consensus cannot be reached. Both consensus views and dissenting views should be recorded. Where issues are too contentious, or effectively non-negotiable (at least for the time being), it will be necessary to state this clearly and to agree when and how an issue may be revisited. There are then many ways of proceeding. For example, work may not proceed further than policy options; thereafter, the highest authority, such as cabinet, may decide how to proceed. In British Columbia, Canada, where a provincial land-use strategy is being negotiated by a large number of interests, decisions revert to government when consensus cannot be reached on issues.

Consensus is not necessary at all stages of the strategy. Indeed, given the value-laden and uncertain nature of many of the issues

and the enormous interests at stake, strong and persistent disagreements are likely. Fundamental differences of value are probably immune to consensus. An exploration and understanding of the diversity of concerns and opinions is very important; and wide participation in the strategy process provides a continuing vehicle for this. Consensus is required (or is desirable) on the objectives and principles of the strategy, on priority issues, and on the best policy responses to priority issues. The process should aim for such consensus. Where it cannot be achieved, future iterations of the strategy should tackle the issues again.

Negotiation

The aim of negotiation is to tackle the trade-offs inherent in sustainable development in order to reach compromise in policy-making or setting responsibilities and plan objectives. It is important at the overall strategy level, and especially in setting decentralized targets. Agreed objectives and targets have a better chance of being implemented than those which are imposed. The processes of negotiation and consensus-building should continue throughout the strategy cycle, so that the strategy can adapt towards continuous improvement. The Netherlands has emphasized negotiation processes for target-setting (Box 10), while UK recycling targets, German carbon dioxide targets, and European Community (EC) sulphur dioxide and

Box 10: Participation in some national strategies

Canada's Green Plan is an example of a government-led consultative process. The plan, an environmental strategy for the federal government, was prepared through the government's budget planning process. It used the existing committee structure, from the Cabinet Committee on the Environment down through committees of deputy and assistant deputy ministers to a management team within the Department of the Environment. A 'multi-stakeholder' advisory committee was set up for the elaborate consultation process, which involved a great many interests: government; business; industry; the environment, youth and indigenous peoples; NGOs; and academics.

A background paper on the plan was released for public consultation, and its contents were substantially revised in light of the consultation; 17 meetings were held with interest group representatives; 41 open public meetings were held; and there was a two-day meeting to consolidate views. Thousands of citizens attended information sessions across the country and contributed suggestions through questionnaires and written submissions. The prescriptions of Canada's Green Plan include: personnel exchanges between NGOs and government; increased support to the Canada Environmental Network; setting up other round tables and advisory councils (on youth and information) (Hill 1993).

The Netherlands' National Environmental Policy Plan is a government-led participatory strategy. It integrates the national land use plan, national transport plan and national energy plan with national planning for agriculture and industry. Such integration has been made possible by multi-disciplinary and participatory approaches. NEPP is intended to relate national policy to local targets. The Netherlands Ministry of Housing, Physical Planning and Environment works with provincial and municipal government and other groups in the NEPP.

Participation has occurred, to varying degrees, in information generation and advice, decision-making and implementation. It is still being developed by government agencies and nine target groups: agricultural producers; the transport sector; chemical manufacturers; gas and electricity suppliers; the construction industry; consumers and retailers; the environmental protection industry; research and educational establishments; and environmental organizations, trade unions and voluntary bodies. Each group is led by a steering committee, consisting of representatives of government and of the target group. Local targets are set by local officials based on the national plan. Provinces are obliged to set targets; municipalities have the incentive of additional central government funding if they also do so. With industry, NEPP has emphasized

box continues

voluntary agreements or covenants to secure agreements with government on environmental objectives and targets. Covenants are negotiated with trades associations, and local variations are allowed for branch members. Ministry staff accept that the price to be paid for a high degree of local participation and motivation will be a certain loss of control over the direction and actions of the NEPP. The ministry has negotiated action plans with all target groups in the NEPP (Hill 1993).

A Platform for Sustainable Development was also established in the Netherlands in 1993 as a forum for agenda-setting and consultation. Members are drawn from many social groups. Debate will be stimulated by campaigns targeted at politicians and the general public; the effectiveness of this presupposes a high degree of participation already existing in the Netherlands — something that is borne out by recent experience.

Nicaragua's National Conservation Strategy involved participation based on the local government structure. Workshops were organized in each of the country's 143 municipalities to make a participatory diagnosis of problems and needs. Short documents summarized the results and were submitted to a second round of workshops — again in every municipality — to decide on proposed actions. Many activities were organized, with groups such as artists, teachers, youth, and political parties, to ensure that a broad range of groups could participate. This helped establish strong links between the strategy and communities and institutions. It also contributed to the national dialogue between antagonists in the recent civil war, and launched locally-driven efforts to solve problems in many parts of Nicaragua.

Nepal's NCS is one of the longest-lived national strategies in Asia, in terms of both participation and implementation. The strategy was closely tied to the National Planning Commission but run as a long-term project. It was decided that the strategy should not initially get too involved in institutional struggles. Key to strategy implementation is a multi-disciplinary, 80-member Environmental Core Group involved in different sectors, although largely from government. From this multi-disciplinary approach sprang a number of participatory exercises in environmental assessment and village planning with villagers and the private sector. User groups were seen as appropriate participants for strategy implementation, as they took a less compartmentalized view than government departments. Hence, for implementation, emphasis was placed on developing the policy context and specific tools to encourage participation of government departments, the private sector and villagers in carrying out EIAs, land use and village plans, for example. This approach of "showing the way by doing" makes the case for institutional change more convincing.

nitrogen oxide targets were set without negotiation. Although the latter targets made a powerful political impact, they have not been met in practice.

The strategy actors and their roles

'Now is the right time to act. But the government acting by itself is insufficient. Government policies that are not owned by the people will not sustain themselves as governments change.'

Gary Lawrence, Sustainable Seattle Initiative

Governments can help provide the right conditions for participation. Initially, however, they are rarely capable of efficiently conducting the necessary participation themselves. Usually, certain changes are desirable to improve participation with successive iterations of the strategy cycle. Governments need to offer conditions conducive to increasing participation. NGOs and local authorities can then take the lead in participation, learn from it, and build their capacity. Governments should build structures and an empowering policy environment to actively support participation; indeed, government itself may conduct certain participation tasks where appropriate and efficient.

Governments

Governments can be highly efficient at running certain strategy tasks with participation – since they can apply many government institutions to the task and can realize economies of scale. Hence, while NGOs may initially play a strong role in acting as catalysts to a new institutional setting with greater participation, this role may become less necessary over time. It is a mistake to think of participation as exclusively an NGO preserve.

A national strategy must involve participation of the major 'horizontal' sectors of the national government, as well as the major 'vertical' divisions, including all the provinces/states and samples of each of the different types of lower level government. Institutional participation of government is therefore important, so that the strategy consensus reflects the views and needs of many government organizations. Also important is the participation of key individuals in government – the kinds of people who can cross barriers and engender vision and change.

The strategy should be able to survive changes in government, and so government participation should be structured accordingly; ie, not overly-dependent on political patronage. Parliamentary and other political processes might be used to ensure cross-party support. The strategies of Victoria (Australia), the Philippines, Nepal and Pakistan are among those that have successfully survived changes in government. In most such cases, the strategy:

Box 11: An important role for local government

In the UK, local authorities are coordinating some of the most innovative sustainable development initiatives in the country. An early local authority environmental audit in the UK — The Green Audit of the county of Lancashire — formed a basis for subsequent participation. It acted as a scene-setter to help begin discussion, as opposed to starting with potentially confrontational dialogue. This led to the participatory Lancashire Environment Forum, a multi-interest group that used the Green Audit to develop the local Agenda 21. The recommendations of this are based on consensus. However, the for-um recognizes that consensus is not immediately possible on everything; as well as defining common positions, the forum also clarifies areas upon which there is not yet agreement — part of the process of setting out the evolving agenda.

In the city of Leicester, there is a strong emphasis on participatory monitoring, to complete the strategy cycle and keep it turning. Public opinion is considered essential for keeping the pressure on; for example, opinion surveys on whether Leicester is getting cleaner are used as a principal basis for the participatory approach.

• is not strongly affiliated to a political party;
• is not entirely in the hands of politicians or civil servants who could be moved by the new government; and
• has strong support outside government.

Usually there are several forms of participatory structures available within the government: the planning systems (town and rural planning tends to have more participatory structures than economic planning, but even so are essentially top-down); the decentralized administrative system; and the education system. These systems have all been used in strategies. Often, however, special committees and round tables have to be set up to increase 'horizontal' participation across interest groups and sectors; not only to ensure that government participation is broad enough, but also to be able to bring in non-governmental inputs. Existing institutional systems are weakest in facilitating these cross-sectoral forms of participation on a continuing basis.

Local government

As Box 11 illustrates, local government can play a key role in implementing strategies. The degree of involvement of local government varies, however, and depends on:

• The size of the country and the number of local governments.

- The stage of the strategy. With each cycle of the strategy, more participants, and hence more local governments can be involved.
- The design of the strategy. For example, the national strategy may be designed to develop gradually from national, to provincial, to local level. Or it may be designed as a national framework, in which local governments and communities can develop their own strategies; the state conservation strategy of Victoria, Australia, provides for municipal strategies (of which there are 24 so far). Or it may start off with the development of local strategies.
- The resources, capacities and political power of local governments.

One way of involving local governments in the early stages of a national strategy is through an association of local governments. This is also an appropriate procedure if resources are limited.

Non-government sectors

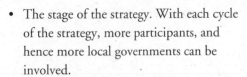

'A key element in the success of the follow-up to Rio is NGO involvement. NGOs have been able to bring in new ideas which would otherwise be kept out.'

Nitin Desai, CSD

In theory, non-government sectors can play significant roles in all elements of the strategy process. They can be full partici-

pants in information collection and analysis, decision-making, implementation, monitoring and adaptation. They can also be advocates and advisers. The roles of non-government sectors will vary greatly between countries, depending on political and social conditions, historical precedents, and their strength and diversity.

Potential non-governmental participants include:

- academic and research institutions;
- associations of resource users (farmers, hunters, fishers, tourism operators, etc);
- banking and financial organizations;
- community groups;
- environmental organizations;
- human development organizations;
- indigenous peoples (some may be involved as governments);
- industry and business (corporate sector);
- the judiciary;
- the media;
- professional associations;
- relief and welfare organizations;
- religious groups;
- schools, teachers, and parent–teacher associations;
- trade unions;
- women's groups;
- international organizations; and
- individual members of the public

Agenda 21 clearly states that non-governmental groups have substantial roles to play in sustainable development. It emphasises that pluralistic civil society, comprising civic groups working alongside government and the private sector, is critical to sustainable development. Non-governmental groups, where truly representative, can be effective in organizing the many niches of civil society; where government recognizes and supports this role financially, technically and legally, the prospects for sustainable development are good.

Until recently, however, governments have tended to dominate strategy processes, perhaps bringing in non-governmental inputs in information collection, in some field implementation and in communication and education processes. For strategies where policy frameworks were prepared with little non-governmental inputs, the value of such involvement has recently been realized, and actively sought in implementation and future iterations of the cycle.

When involving non-governmental interest groups – NGOs, community groups, the private sector, etc – care has to be taken to ensure the representativeness and accountability of these groups. This is particularly the case in making the key decisions of the strategy.

Representativeness: How representative of the interest is the participating group? An apparently single interest may in fact consist of several competing interests. The fishing sector, for example, may be divided into industrial fishing, artisanal fishing, and recreational fishing, and may be further divided by catch or gear (for example, crab fishing, shrimp fishing, trawling, purse seining). To provide a fair reflection of the fishing sector, representation should come from all these interests. If complete representation of a sector is not possible (and it seldom is), participants in the strategy should be aware of those interests not being reflected and how their concerns differ from those of the 'representative' group.

Accountability: How accountable are the individuals to their interest group? For example, the terms of reference of the Steering Committee and other committees and working groups should state whether members are there in their personal capacity or as representatives of a particular group. In the latter case, there must be a mechanism by which the representative is accountable to the group, reports to it, and receives instructions from it. This is not difficult to achieve when the interest group is represented by an association with democratic procedures, such as a national chamber of commerce, an association of municipalities, or a professional association. It is more difficult when a coalition or temporary association has to be put together expressly to participate in the strategy.

Fairness: Are all interest groups equally well-equipped to participate, in terms of time, money, skills and access to information? National and provincial government officials are paid to participate and usually have ready access to information. Most large corporations have the resources needed to attend meetings, analyze papers, and collect data. Many small businesses, community groups and environmental and social interest groups do not have these resources. To be on an equal footing with wealthier and more powerful participants, they need financial and sometimes technical support to attend meetings and prepare informed positions. Some governments have introduced special funding programmes for this purpose. Unfortunately, these can be expensive, particularly when many interest groups are involved. But not always; in Nepal, the NCS process includes a special NGO support programme which facilitates these contributions to strategy implementation. As little as US$1000 and focused technical help can ensure long-term input and mount a community project.

These three principles – representativeness, accountability and fairness – are difficult to maintain in practice. A reasonable aim is for as much of each as possible, within the constraints of budgets, timetables set by political deadlines, and capacity to manage a logistically complex process.

NGOs

NGOs are diverse; and proliferate in types and numbers. They cover a spectrum from long-established, major international and national institutions to fragile, local operations with no staff or guaranteed funding. They may work on single issues, or broad-based development concerns. Almost all operate through organizing groups of people to make better use of their own resource.

The United Nations (UN) uses a broad definition of NGOs, to include non-profit organizations in the private sector, academic and research organizations and local government. This broader scope is reflected in the term much-used by Agenda 21: the 'major groups' or the 'independent sectors'. NGOs are also known as the 'third sector' in contrast to the government and business sectors.

'The vast majority of the [NGO] bodies are national or local in nature, and a successful transition to sustainable development will require substantial strengthening of their capacities.'

WCED 1987

Agenda 21 calls on governments to draw on the 'expertise and views of NGOs' for sustainable development. NGO expertise and views encompass many practical functions:

- mobilizing the public, or certain groups;
- detailed field knowledge of social and environmental conditions;
- delivery of services (disaster relief, education, health);
- encouraging appropriate community

organization and capacity building;
- research, policy analysis and advice;
- facilitation and improvement of social and political processes;
- mediation and reconciliation of conflict;
- awareness-raising and communications;
- watchdog, warning and monitoring;
- advocacy and challenging the status quo; promoting alternatives; and
- training in, and use of, participatory approaches.

These functions are often complementary to government and the private sector, and can be exercised by individual NGOs or by partnerships and networks.

NGO coalitions can complement and buttress weak governments. This is common, for example, in the case of welfare and in engagement with local communities, where institutional constraints mean that governments are limited in their capacity to use participatory methods. On the other hand, NGO coalitions can act as a check and critic where governments and the private sector are too strong (for example, appropriating natural resources and causing adverse social and environmental impacts).

NCSs or NEAPs have tended to involve environmental NGOs more than other types. In contrast, sustainable development strategies aim to deal more extensively with the social dimension, in which development NGOs or community-based organizations (CBOs) have much experience. This is

particularly the case as strategies address the common policy/planning system failure to link government to local communities and resource users; understand and act on local complexity; and enlist local resource users in implementation. All of these are areas where NGOs have comparative advantages: at the middle level between central government and local communities.

To date, national strategies show no standard pattern of NGO involvement. Governments have almost always been dominant in strategy processes and their outcomes. In some instances, outside agencies have had to ensure that local NGOs were formally involved. In Indonesia, Togo, Kenya and Rwanda, for example, the World Bank was responsible for initiating tripartite government/NGO/Bank meetings on sectoral and national development strategies.

Occasionally NGOs can play central roles in sustainable development in a government vacuum. In Kenya and Tanzania, for example, NGOs operate a major proportion of the health system. In Northern Pakistan, the Aga Khan Rural Support Programme (AKRSP) is the leading actor in rural development support. The Bangladesh Rural Advancement Centre (BRAC) runs a large proportion of that country's primary schools. These major operations are the exception. Yet their much-publicized success tends to have resulted in NGOs being viewed principally as 'delivery mechanisms' – or worse, as amateurs – rather than as

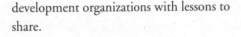

development organizations with lessons to share.

Last, it must be remembered that NGOs do not act as one group. With respect to sustainable development, they cover a range of approaches:

- 'interest'-based NGOs, eg, natural history societies and professional associations;
- 'concern'-based NGOs, eg, environmental and animal welfare campaigning and advocacy groups; and
- 'solution'-based NGOs, eg, education and rural development groups.

It is the type of approach, as much as the function of the NGO, that will really determine how it can participate in a strategy. Many NGOs, particularly the solution-based groups, are comfortable with ideas of participation and consensus and actively promote them. Others, who work through lobbying and advocacy, tend to see their role as one of 'disagreeing', and prefer not to seek compromise. A few of these NGOs (particularly from environmental and welfare campaigning interests) therefore have taken approaches which appear to be incompatible with sustainable development, which depends upon negotiated trade-offs. Normally, such NGOs will stay on the margins of a participatory strategy. In such a strategy, the debate and consensus will take place within a middle ground; nonetheless, it should seek to involve all sectors and major groups.

The private sector

It is important to seek representative, accountable members of the private sector (trades and industry associations, local chambers of commerce and industry and the trade unions, etc). Usually, however, it is also effective to bring in the private sector leaders who are responsible for forming new patterns of investment and operation in the country. This is the approach of the (global) Business Council for Sustainable Development (BCSD), Round Table structures in Canada, and in the Pakistan NCS.

Private sector involvement tends to mean that big business and industry, (ie those responsible for much of the resource use, waste creation and employment), are often important participants. However, this should not exclude the involvement of socially-significant smaller-scale industries which may be important for employment (the approach of Ireland); smaller businesses with particularly high resource requirements (for example, small-scale mining, or forest/ agricultural processing); or those industries with particularly sensitive environmental impacts (for example, tourism). National strategies in Germany and the Netherlands have programmes of intensive negotiations among industry associations, unions and the appropriate level of government to decide on operating standards and targets.

Direct involvement with communities and individuals

The local level is the most practical one for public participation, in the sense of involving individuals directly rather than through organizations. Few governments – or individuals for that matter – can afford the same degree of participation at state or national levels that can be achieved locally. If it is not practical to involve every community – and in national strategies it usually is not – a method of sampling communities will be needed. This should ensure that participating communities are reasonably representative of the diversity of communities in the country, the communities most affected by the priority issues, all geographical regions, ecological zones and livelihood types. Furthermore, the sampling methods should, of course, be able to obtain information and insights from the whole community – not just the leaders – and particularly from those who are in some way marginalized.

It is often difficult to sustain community interest in processes that take a long time. Loss of interest is inevitable if the strategy appears removed from people's more pressing daily concerns. On the other hand, community strategies that meet people's needs will attract and retain support for a long time. In general, the sooner the national strategy is complemented by local strategies and other local activities, the better. There is also a strong argument for undertaking a range of demonstration local strategies from the outset in a national strategy as a way of feeding and testing policies.

Planning for participation

Different types, and different degrees, of participation are needed for each strategy task, and for each phase or cycle of strategy development. These must be planned for, based on the following factors:

Definition of strategy theme

The likely 'parcel' of main issues to be dealt with together needs to be elaborated. It may amount to, for example:

- sectoral environmental concerns;
- cross-sectoral environmental concerns; and
- comprehensive sustainable development concerns (where these cover significant social issues, they will generally demand more participation than strictly environmental concerns).

Definition of strategy level

It needs to be decided at which main levels policy and institutional change are required to address the above issues. These will usually be:

- national;
- provincial; or

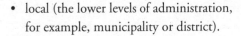

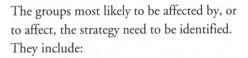

- local (the lower levels of administration, for example, municipality or district).

However, often the key to effective change will be to link one or more levels; for example, a national strategy must not be thought of as entirely a national-level exercise.

Stakeholder analysis

The groups most likely to be affected by, or to affect, the strategy need to be identified. They include:

- government;
- resource user groups;
- local government;
- consumer groups;
- NGOs;
- traditional community groups;
- academics;
- business;
- religious/cultural groups;
- unions;
- communities; and
- eminent persons.

The definition of strategy theme and level, and stakeholder analysis, should be carried out at the same time. Together, they will help to refine the strategy objectives and approach, in particular the choice of participation structures and methodologies, and incentives required for participation.

Choice of participation structures and methodologies

The general range of participation structures and methods suitable for a given strategy will depend upon its theme and level, and the stakeholders in the process.

The particular participation method used at any time within the strategy will depend on:

- the specific strategy task (eg, information collection, analysis, decision-making, implementation, monitoring); and
- the maturity of the strategy (the number of times the strategy has gone through its cycle).

Structures available for participation: For most strategy tasks, the promising structures tend to be: the planning system; traditional structures (for example, village-based systems, religious systems); and specially-constituted committees, round tables and core groups and networks. For communications, information, education and monitoring tasks, the useful structures are: the education system, extension system, the arts/theatre, and the media.

Participation methodologies: For survey, analysis and monitoring tasks, useful approaches include:

- participatory inquiry (Box 9);
- resource surveys; and
- 'green' audits.

Box 12: Why is it difficult to institutionalize participation?

Why is participation so difficult to institutionalize, if it has so many intrinsic merits? The following seem to be the key constraints:

- In the initial phases of a strategy, participation requires considerable time and extra effort in development of human resources. Generally no extra incentives are provided to the staff members for the extra effort required. To introduce participation requires more financial resources and is more costly compared to conventional programmes in the initial phase. Most institutions and programmes feel constrained in making such investments since they are evaluated primarily by the criteria of achievement of physical and financial targets.

- Participation requires major reversals in the role of external professionals, from "management" to facilitation. This requires changes in behaviour and attitudes, and can only be gradual. It requires significant retraining but, usually, inadequate resources are devoted to training.

- Participation also threatens conventional careers; professionals feel a loss of power in dealing with local communities as equals and including them in decision-making. This discourages professionals from taking risks and developing collaborative relationships with communities.

- Participation and institutional development are difficult to measure and require using quantitative and qualitative performance indicators together. Existing monitoring and evaluation systems cannot measure these well; thus, physical and financial indicators, which are easier to measure, dominate the performance evaluation and impact analysis process.

- While many programmes initiated by external agencies tend to use participatory methods for planning, they do not make corresponding changes in resource allocation mechanisms to local institutions, and they tend to retain financial decision-making powers for themselves. This hampers the growth of local institutions and leads to poor sustainability of the programmes.

- Participation is a long drawn-out process and needs to be iterative in the initial period of two to five years before being scaled up and replicated. Most development programmes tend to blueprint the process of participation and institution building in the early phases without enough experimentation and iteration. As a result, the institutional forms which evolve are often ineffective.

box continues

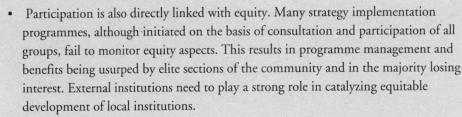

- Participation is also directly linked with equity. Many strategy implementation programmes, although initiated on the basis of consultation and participation of all groups, fail to monitor equity aspects. This results in programme management and benefits being usurped by elite sections of the community and in the majority losing interest. External institutions need to play a strong role in catalyzing equitable development of local institutions.

Any policy or strategy formulation process should take stock of existing efforts at local level, and use them as building blocks for strategy preparation. The process of strategy formulation has an important bearing on its successful implementation. Organic growth of a strat-egy through local and regional inputs, based on action and learning from results, increases the chances of all the stakeholders developing a long-term interest in implementation.

Source: Shah (1994)

For policy formulation and decision-making tasks:

- consensus-building;
- negotiation; and
- traditional methods, for example, of conflict resolution.

For implementation tasks:

- voluntary agreements; and
- joint management.

For communications, information, education and monitoring tasks:

- seminars;
- workshops;
- interviews; and
- exhibitions and plays.

The government planning and administration structure and the political structure will largely determine whether it is possible for a national strategy to be built up from local initiatives, or whether the initiative has to start from the top, and filter down through participation and existing decentralization structures. It will also partly determine what kind of mix of participatory and multi-disciplinary approaches can be taken. In Uganda, for example, the government's decentralization policy allowed strong inputs from most of the 38 districts in the strategy (through consultations and three-day workshops) although the results have been selectively used at central government level. Some key constraints to institutionalizing participation are discussed in Box 12.

It is important at the outset that strategy participants know how far up the decision-making hierarchies their recommendations can and will reach. One of the failures of participation has been disillusionment resulting from unrealistic expectations about its impact on policies and actions.

Scheduling and resources required

A phased approach to participation is likely to be best, beginning with the use of participation structures and methodologies with which the majority of participants are familiar. They should also be acceptable scientifically (trustworthiness criteria are available for participatory techniques as well as for 'scientific' approaches) and politically (representativeness and accountability). It is very difficult to bring about intensive consultation with all the stakeholder groups in an initial strategy cycle. As with the scope of the strategy, it is best to build up to greater ambitions; otherwise the strategy runs the risk of being overwhelmed. The capacity for participation can be built throughout the process; indeed, participation has been instrumental in much of the capacity-building of many successful national and local strategies.

Linking levels of strategy experience

It is important to link national-level strategy experience with local-level participation experience. Participation in strategies can have both 'horizontal' and 'vertical' reach. Horizontal participation is required across sectoral interest groups, government ministries, and communities in different parts of the country, to ensure that impacts across sectors or regions are dealt with. Vertical participation is required to facilitate a two-way flow of influence and to address problems that are experienced farther down the hierarchy; from national to local levels, or from leaders right down to marginalized groups and individuals. Vertical participation is also required because localized activities will lead to cumulative problems experienced farther up the hierarchy.

Recent national strategies have tended to concentrate on horizontal participation, with extensive government and academic contributions at national level. Much multi-disciplinary analysis has been undertaken, and policies have been changed, often extensively – at least on paper. In almost all of the strategies, there was relatively little participation initially. However, as a result of these strategies there were, in many cases, strong recommendations for participation in subsequent local strategy planning, implementation and monitoring (see Box 10). Although there have been some improvements to national-level government institutions and some regulatory instruments have been introduced, there has generally been little impact so far on the ground. There appear to be many local blocks to implementation.

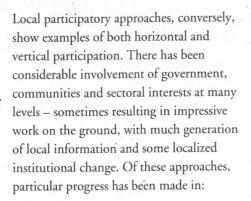

Local participatory approaches, conversely, show examples of both horizontal and vertical participation. There has been considerable involvement of government, communities and sectoral interests at many levels – sometimes resulting in impressive work on the ground, with much generation of local information and some localized institutional change. Of these approaches, particular progress has been made in:

- joint community/business/local government initiatives in urban or peri-urban areas, often catalyzed by local governments and NGOs – for example, Groundwork UK, local Agenda 21s undertaken by Australian and UK local authorities;
- buffer zones (economic support zones) around national parks, with joint government/community planning and action, including many well-documented examples, for example, in India, Nepal and Zimbabwe; and
- extensive rural development projects based upon social organization and/or environmental protection, often at watershed and river basin level, again catalyzed and/or managed by NGOs, for example, the AKRSP in India and North Pakistan.

Although most did not start as local strategies, many of these successful local projects have had to evolve strategic approaches to thrive, linking with national policy and institutional initiatives.

In spite of individual successes, the problem of 'scaling up' such local participatory initiatives remains plagued by policy and institutional inertia. In many instances, it may be necessary for government departments to sort out their own differences – using multi-disciplinary approaches – before embarking on full-scale participation. In Australia, the very different approaches of federal, state and municipal strategies have necessitated an Inter-governmental Agreement on the Environment to ensure consistency among them; this has had the effect of putting the federal strategy in the ascendancy.

A number of approaches have managed to make the leap from participation at local level to national level; for example, Gestion de Terroir in the Sahel, which has always addressed the administrative and legal constraints to local activity, and which gradually builds up a larger, national-level presence. The AKRSP in Northern Pakistan has led to a major government-led National Rural Support Programme. This may have been influenced by the fact that AKRSP staff also played key roles in the Pakistan NCS.

In general, however, we know that the genesis and implementation of national strategies and local participatory efforts have tended to be very separate. Furthermore, there have been few efforts to unite them to their mutual advantage. The successful harmonization of national strategies and local participatory efforts will be dependent on the following factors.

Building on existing participatory structures, methods and projects

There must be a conscious effort by national strategy coordinators to improve top-down and bottom-up approaches. A variety of actors and structures can be used to explore possible existing links, including NGOs and local authorities, traditional structures, specially-formed committees and round tables, and major sustainable development projects.

Alternatively, new methods for forging links could be adopted, including participatory inquiry, voluntary agreements and joint management.

Capacity-building

At the policy level, capacity is needed to deal with the rich insights and information coming from local participatory approaches, to devolve appropriate power to participating partners, and to monitor the impacts. At the local level, capacity is needed to take up the challenges that newer policies offer. It is becoming increasingly clear, however, that it is at the middle level – the province or municipality – where capacity-building can reap the most benefits. At this level, there is much potential to link top levels (where policy is set) and bottom levels (where policy is implemented, and from where policy-relevant information is required).

Public information, education and communication

Public information, education and communications (IEC) activities are integral to the entire strategy process because:

- they keep participants informed of progress with the strategy, through all tasks and phases and from cycle to cycle;
- they provide a consensus expression of the strategy—particularly the policy framework and action plans; and
- they help implement and monitor the strategy by generating a wider understanding of strategy goals and how to achieve them; encouraging participation in, support for, and feedback on the strategy; and leading to behaviour change.

The most appropriate IEC activities will vary with each strategy: Box 13 gives some key questions which can help determine optimum communications strategies.

Keeping participants informed of strategy progress

During all phases of the strategy, the secretariat can act as a clearing house for communications; for example, organizing workshops and briefings, publishing a newsletter of strategy activities, reporting on progress to different groups, and maintaining an information base. In addition to issuing press releases, regular briefings of the media will be needed. Certain activities will

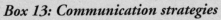

Box 13: Communication strategies

The National Institute of Design in India has defined a sequence of eight questions which it follows in the field when developing communications strategies for national or local development programmes. This approach has been tested and refined through more than a decade of field experience. The eight key questions to ask are:

1. **Target audience:** whose behaviour must communication attempt to change?

2. **Target response:** what is the behaviour change that is needed?

3. **Research involved:** what do we need to know about existing knowledge, attitudes and practices before planning our messages?

4. **Target message:** what messages can be exchanged between planners/activists and target audiences to help achieve the desired response?

5. **Media:** what media are best suited to the exchange of the target message?

6. **Media resource institutions and individuals:** what skills and talent can be drawn upon to help develop and implement media decisions?

7. **Budget:** what will be the cost of communication plans to reach each target audience?

8. **Evaluation criteria:** what goals and indicators will be used to monitor the intended behaviour change?

Evaluation should lead to reviewing each step in a sequence, and reactivating the sequence in the next phase of the communications strategy.

be more specific to given strategy tasks and cycles:

- **Building commitment to the strategy:** Early priority should be given to communicating the purpose, objectives, work plans, and likely benefits of the strategy; and to setting up working links with the communication facilities of specific participant groups and the media. Videos (Botswana and Pakistan) and well-presented strategy 'prospectus' briefing documents (Nepal and Zambia) have been used successfully.

- **Strategy analysis and policy formulation:** Major contributors to the strategy will need to be accessible (for interviews, press briefings, lecture circuits), to enlarge the immediate strategy constituency. Public debate on draft findings and emerging options can be encouraged in both the mass media and traditional media. Journalists have played strong roles in some strategies, such as Pakistan's.

- **Action planning and budgeting:** Networks of education and 'extension' agents can be set in place, according to the field requirements of the action plan. Such communications agents will be required as much for industry and businesses as for rural resource users and the resource-consuming public.

- **Implementation:** The various implementing agencies will run their own communications programmes (with the media having established its role as critic and monitor), encouraging the public to play similar roles in pushing for, and monitoring, standards and indicators of sustainability. A strategy communications clearing house may still be required. This could be linked to the information resources centre required for strategy planning work. The clearing house coordinator may organize awareness campaigns, specialized seminars, training sessions, briefings, etc, for the various communications agents.

Consensus expressions of the strategy

The common practice of referring to the strategy document as 'the strategy' is misleading and encourages people to spend excessive efforts preparing documents instead of developing and implementing the strategy. Documents are only intermediate products of the process.

Strategy documents, covering at least the policy frameworks and action plans, are essential nonetheless, so that all participants know what was agreed to and what is expected of them. Without documents, the strategy may quickly lose coherence and break up into ad hoc decisions dictated by the immediate needs of the agencies concerned. The documents need not be too lengthy, however. Coherence, consensus and clear direction are important features of a strategy and the documents will need to express these features, while providing an overall framework. Other components of the strategy, such as the investment portfolio, may require longer and more detailed documentation.

To be most effective, the central strategy document needs to be published and widely available in its approved form. Government agencies, local authorities, major NGOs and many businesses will need the full document. But highly technical reports are not useful for politicians and busy decision-makers. High quality, clear, concise documents written in everyday language, with charts, maps and illustrations, should be used for these groups. The main strategy documents may need to be in several different forms, each targeted to a particular audience.

Condensed information can be made available to the public – in local languages where appropriate – and to schools and universities, the latter highlighting educa-

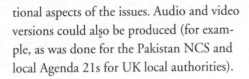

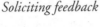

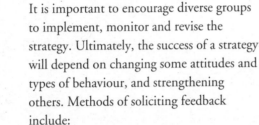

tional aspects of the issues. Audio and video versions could also be produced (for example, as was done for the Pakistan NCS and local Agenda 21s for UK local authorities).

Soliciting feedback

It is important to encourage diverse groups to implement, monitor and revise the strategy. Ultimately, the success of a strategy will depend on changing some attitudes and types of behaviour, and strengthening others. Methods of soliciting feedback include:

- **Public relations activities:** these tend to have a short-term impact, and are principally one-way communications. They can be conducted through the mass media and advertising.
- **Public awareness activities:** these have a medium-term impact. They work by consulting groups in the strategy process, through traditional and mass media and government/NGO participation structures; involving them in the debate on sustainable development, and keeping them informed about all aspects of the outcomes.
- **Public participation:** this has a longer-term impact, and takes a much longer time. It depends upon incentives, formal and informal education and training, and results in behaviourial change. Mass media activities are much less significant here. Active participation and experience are key, particularly in setting and

monitoring indicators of sustainable development.

An IEC plan will be needed. It should identify key participants/audiences, topics and means of communicating them, and roles in IEC. The plan will obviously be revised and more detailed once strategy implementation begins; the Pakistan NCS devotes a whole chapter to the communications strategy.

Skills in planning and running an IEC programme will be vital; as will training, where these are in short supply. The IEC team will need to understand the conceptual basis, genesis and dynamics of the strategy, as well as the technical issues. A priority task for the IEC team will be to set up a network of principal communications agents and media for different localities, topics and groups.

Choice of media

Effective media communication will empower individuals and groups, enabling them to use their skills and resources and identify new ways of working together. The media should, therefore, enable participating groups to communicate what they feel, what they know, and what they want. Accordingly, successful communication cannot be solely a one-way media campaign, but must be a two-way process of information exchange and learning. The key will be in linking participants with appropriate media.

The most effective media for communication will differ according to country and locality circumstances, topic, audience/participant group and cost considerations. Mass media should be seen as a supplement to, and not a substitute for, other media and public information and education in the process of behaviour change. We have become accustomed to thinking of mass media as prime agents of change. They can and do contribute to change, and they have importance in raising the awareness of the general public and in influencing key decision-makers and opinion-formers. Yet, the real change must take place at the local, community and individual level – and here 'mass' approaches are of limited relevance.

In many low-income areas, print and electronic media may not be appropriate for most participants; here, person-to-person communication (including entertainment and performing arts) may have greater impact. Agricultural extension agents – if generally effective – will also need to be involved.

When creating a strategy constituency in the print, electronic and traditional media, and in the education system, it will be important not to restrict the role of these various media to delivering strategy 'messages'. Where socio-political conditions allow, media roles should encompass those of strategy critic, monitor, and solicitor of opinions.

Conclusion

One of the major challenges facing many strategies is to increase the level and effectiveness of participation. The constraints to participation outlined in Box 12 need particular attention. Priority may be given to:

- institutional reviews of the main agencies that should be promoting and supporting participation;
- training in participatory methods;
- close monitoring of early participation exercises – and particularly of their risks; and
- promotion at high levels of the real impacts of participation.

Strategies based fully upon participation will find that their institutional framework, management and cost structure begin to change in line with the trends listed in Box 8. The national strategy secretariat and task force, for example, may be complemented by local groups, which come to take a lead in further iterations of the strategy. Strategy teams may increasingly bring in people who have been active in participatory projects, but who so far have had little to do with the strategy process. National planning procedures may better accommodate multi-actor approaches, and previously marginalized groups may share platforms with recognized authorities.

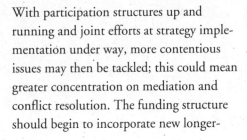

With participation structures up and running and joint efforts at strategy implementation under way, more contentious issues may then be tackled; this could mean greater concentration on mediation and conflict resolution. The funding structure should begin to incorporate new longer-term provisions for joint action, such as trust funds for community initiatives. All of this will have major implications for the way that strategies are managed. The critical mass of effort should then begin to turn away from national strategies and toward local strategies.

PART 2

The Strategy Cycle

Chapter 6

Getting Started

Strategies for sustainable development need to build on and provide a framework for other forms of strategy processes operating at national level. Once the concept of the strategy as an adaptive and cyclical process has been embraced, then, whether a biodiversity action plan, national Agenda 21, World Bank NEAP, or other multi-sectoral process, it is likely to have similar management needs.

The strategy process should include information assembly and analysis, policy formulation, action planning, implementation, and monitoring and evaluation. Each of these components is driven and facilitated by participation and communication. A multi-track process, in which most of the strategy components occur simultaneously, is likely to be more effective than a single-track process in which most occur sequentially. The strategy experience to date has usually followed a sequential approach without fully appreciating the central functions of communication and participation. Inevitably, a multi-track process including working links between the various components and continual reflection and revision will be a more complex management process demanding a broader range of skills than the more conventional approach.

The basic management structure or engine for most strategies has been a steering committee and secretariat and, although they have come in many shapes and sizes, experience suggests some general rules for their functions, location, status and composition. The start-up phase of a strategy can be a time of some frustration while relationships with existing activities are thought through, key participants (including donors) brought on board, decisions are made and the basic directions set from a range of options. Well-targeted, decisive but diplomatic management at this early stage can determine the level of success of the strategy in later phases.

The first steps

Once the political decision has been made to begin a strategy, the main participants need to have a shared understanding of the way forward. These participants include, at the least, the small group of government agencies, and possibly NGOs, which will be taking the primary responsibility for managing the process. Awareness may have built up during preliminary discussions of a possible strategy, but in some cases, these will have involved only a few influential administrators and politicians. It can be useful at this stage for a lead government agency to conduct a round of briefing meetings within and outside government on the nature of strategies and the steps the government now intends to take to get the process going.

Prior to the establishment of some formal structure for managing the strategy process, some uncertainty is to be expected, the extent of which will depend largely on the original source of the strategy initiative. This source can determine the initial management approach; although, as the managers of the strategy gain confidence and the process gains momentum, its origin fades in importance. Strategies that have departed from the original model to truly express national identity have tended to be the most successful.

The elements, structures and resources required for the management process will be generic to all strategies, be they:

- a precondition to receiving World Bank loans (110 borrower countries find themselves in this position);
- a global strategy such as Caring for the Earth or the Brundtland Commission Report;
- legal obligations under global conventions such as the Biodiversity or Climate Change agreements;
- global strategies of a sectoral or thematic nature such as those on tropical forestry and desertification which, when expressed nationally, have expanded to have multi-sectoral dimensions; or,
- previous or existing sub-national strategy initiatives.

Attracting funding and support

In some developing countries, the decision to proceed with a strategy has not met with external funding support and the initiative has gone no further. The decision to go ahead may have been made by a single ministry (often an environmental ministry), but without the critical mass of commitment within government that would ensure the redistribution of internal resources to support the process at the outset.

Early NCSs were often confronted with these initial resource constraints. Kenya, for example, was one of the first countries to express an interest in undertaking an NCS, but IUCN, as the external technical support organization, could not muster the resources. During the early 1980s, IUCN had

some 15 countries on record as having made
formal requests for assistance to initiate
conservation strategies. Resources for these
were never found. In other countries like
Nigeria, Zimbabwe and Ethiopia, where the
decision to proceed with an NCS was
accompanied by internal commitments of
technical expertise and funds, this hiatus did
not occur.

Even where resources have been available,
difficult decisions on how best to proceed
can still delay start-up. Guidance from an
external technical agency, which can draw
from extensive strategy experience, can be
essential in the start-up phase. Once a
decision to undertake a strategy has been
made, the first step for a government is
forging partnerships between donors and an
appropriate technical support agency. This
negotiation process can take some time;
extending well over a year for the Bangladesh, Vietnam and Tanzania NCSs.

Case studies of strategies in Asia, Africa and
Latin America (IUCN, 1994 A,B,C) show
that the problem of attracting necessary
resources in a timely way to build on government commitment has plagued NCSs at
all phases of their development. World Bank
NEAPs in Africa, on the other hand, have
been remarkable for the efficiency with
which they get up and running. There are a
number of very good reasons for this, which
provide lessons for the future:

- Most NEAPs have only recently been
  initiated (since 1992) and have benefitted
  from a decade of strategy experience.
- The World Bank has the authority and
  leverage to require governments to give
  priority to the NEAP process.
- The Bank has come with the NEAP
  requirement at the same time as their
  guarantee of start-up seed funding.
- The Bank supports a series of consultant
  technical missions leading up to and
  following the decision to proceed with an
  NEAP. These prepare much of the early
  design documentation (even drafting
  cabinet submissions on occasions),
  facilitate consultation, and provide
  backing to the establishment and early
  operation of the NEAP secretariat.
- The Bank uses its central position in the
  economy of many countries and its close
  relation with UNDP to draw in other
  donors to support the NEAP process.

Although efficacious in getting NEAP
management under way, the World Bank
approach can have its costs, as discussed in
Chapter 10. The key to good strategy
management is ensuring that the process
proceeds at a pace and in a form which best
suits local conditions and which is most
sensitive to existing capacities.

The relationship of the initiative with other
strategies, either underway or under consideration, is another factor that causes
uncertainty during the period of the initial
decision. A country may have embarked on

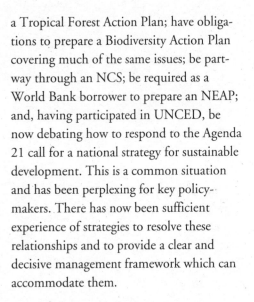

a Tropical Forest Action Plan; have obligations to prepare a Biodiversity Action Plan covering much of the same issues; be part-way through an NCS; be required as a World Bank borrower to prepare an NEAP; and, having participated in UNCED, be now debating how to respond to the Agenda 21 call for a national strategy for sustainable development. This is a common situation and has been perplexing for key policy-makers. There has now been sufficient experience of strategies to resolve these relationships and to provide a clear and decisive management framework which can accommodate them.

Strategies as cyclical processes

The strategy cycle consists of the following:

- information assembly and analysis;
- policy formulation;
- action planning (and budgeting);
- implementation, including capacity building;
- monitoring and evaluation; and
- review, revision and adaption.

The separation and sequence of these elements is somewhat arbitrary. As the strategy progresses, assessment (information assembly and analysis) and policy formulation are likely to be a part of implementation that best starts from the earliest stages. Participation and communication are driving forces of all elements of the process.

With many strategies, information assembly and analysis, policy formulation, action planning, and document preparation have followed one another, and have been concentrated largely in a preparation phase. Capacity-building, implementation, and monitoring and evaluation have been concentrated in an implementation phase.

In this approach to a strategy process, many of the elements are sequential, as if following each other along a single track. Figure 3 gives an example.

There are several drawbacks to this single-track approach. First, it encourages an excessive emphasis on the preparation of a strategy document, and an investment in information assembly, policy formulation and planning quite out of proportion to what can be implemented. This is likely to reinforce any existing prejudice that strategies are academic and irrelevant to the real business of government and society. The multiple steps under policy formulation and action planning are usual during the initial development (preparation) of the strategy policies and action plan, but may not be necessary in subsequent cycles.

Second, it fosters a view of strategies as linear rather than cyclical. In the single-track model, there is no commitment to regular review and revision of the policy framework for the strategy as an essential component of a country's development cycle. It is viewed more as a one-off event.

Figure 3: An example of a single-track strategy process

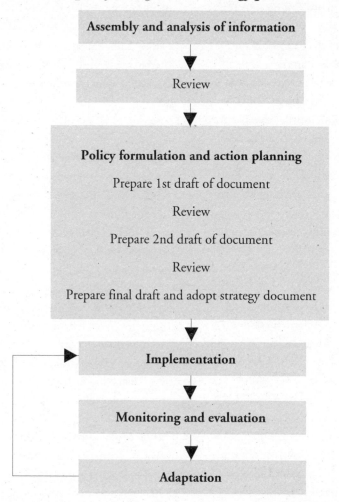

Third, it denies the strategy one of its strongest assets: its ability to focus on the elements of the process that will have the greatest strategic effect at a particular point in time. For example, communication of certain messages may be most important at one point, and capacity-building most important at another.

Finally, the single-track approach does not reflect what is needed. Participation, information assembly and analysis, communication, and monitoring are continuous process elements needed throughout the life of the strategy. Evaluation, policy formulation and action planning will need to occur regularly in each process cycle. Implementation can take place at the same time as policy formulation and action planning.

In many cases one of the first needs is to build the capacity to undertake a strategy; until this is done, the rest of the strategy process is either halted or has to be developed by outsiders. Recognizing this, a number of strategies – in Bhutan and Guinea-Bissau, for example – have begun with capacity-building: the formation of a team, the training of that team on a project (such as organization of a core group to develop environmental assessment procedures) or a thematic or regional strategy.

Early implementation of those aspects of the strategy for which commitment has been obtained also helps to prevent a common problem with many strategies so far: a hiatus between the main preparation phase of a strategy and the main implementation. The more the division between preparation and implementation phase can be overcome, the more confident participants will be that the strategy justifies their commitment of time, energy and money. Demonstration projects can be particularly helpful to this end.

Consequently, a multi-track approach is likely to offer the most practical form of strategy process. In this approach, many (but not necessarily all) of the elements are undertaken simultaneously. Figure 4 illustrates the strategy cycle.

Using the term 'multi-track' is still a little misleading. It implies that the tracks do not meet and ignores the need for feedback. In practice, there will be feedback among the different elements of the strategy process, each influencing the others.

In addition, there will be feedback between one phase or cycle of the strategy and another. This feedback will occur through effective monitoring and evaluation. Feedback will need to reflect how the strategy influences and is influenced by events, such as changes in attitudes and behaviour, markets and prices, population growth, and environmental conditions.

Thus, a 'picture' of a strategy would not be a long line, or even a set of long lines, stretching into the future. It would more likely be a spiral of lines indicating activities and feedback loops that progressively approach the goal.

There are, of course, many possible versions of this approach. There is no single correct way of managing a strategy. The need is to be pragmatic and incremental; aiming not for perfection but for constant improvement. The cyclical nature of a strategy, whereby each element of the process may be repeated several times, means that the strategy can start off quite modestly, gradually becoming more ambitious.

For example, participation in the strategy needs eventually to be both wide and deep,

Figure 4: The strategy cycle

This figure shows the elements of the strategy as a series of consecutive steps. In reality, many elements will occur concurrently, ie implementation of various kinds and capacity building need to continue throughout the cycle.

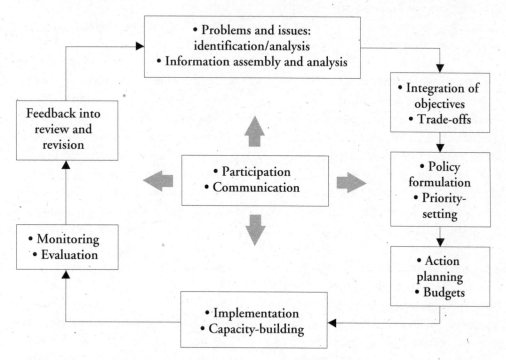

involving many people in all sectors of society. If a strategy were to start off by attempting to involve everybody, however, it would quickly become bogged down and exhaust its resources. Participation in the first cycle of the strategy may involve only a few key sectors of society but can be widened and deepened as the strategy develops.

Inevitably, strategies are processes which require optimization, opportunism, and often muddling through in complicated administrative and political environments. Because of their complexity, strategies must cater to and involve many interests, and offer mechanisms for defining and agreeing on trade-offs. Like all processes that determine how resources should be used and by whom, strategies are constantly subject to political forces. These are necessary and useful influences, so long as the strategy secretariat adheres to an open process and is flexible; seeking to capitalize on opportunities as they arise to promote agreed strategy objectives.

The strategy should be designed to influence the development process and decision-

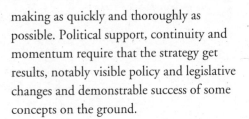

making as quickly and thoroughly as possible. Political support, continuity and momentum require that the strategy get results, notably visible policy and legislative changes and demonstrable success of some concepts on the ground.

Process management

The large number of process elements, their specific technical requirements, and the number of participants in a strategy call for good process management. Regardless of where the strategy is in its cycle, two bodies are usually required for this: a steering committee and a strategy secretariat.

The main tasks of these bodies are to coordinate, facilitate and support the work of the participants; ie, the organizations within and outside government who prepare and implement the strategy. The steering committee and secretariat also may have to undertake some of the strategy tasks themselves to get it going, to demonstrate and test policies, or to execute a major change in scope or direction. But the strategy will be pointless if it is regarded as belonging to the steering committee and secretariat rather than as being a central concern and activity of the rest of government and society.

As facilitating and coordinating bodies, neither the steering committee nor the secretariat should have vested interests in a sector, or be located within a sector or interest group. This usually means that they have to be specially constituted, unless an NCS, NEAP or other type of strategy with an existing steering committee and secretariat is already in progress.

They should be located where they can have the greatest influence on the national development system. This may be in the office of the President or Prime Minister, a Ministry of Economic Planning, or an independent office directly linked to the cabinet or a powerful cabinet body. Locating the steering committee and secretariat in a line ministry is less desirable. It could identify them too much with the ministry concerned, and result in the strategy being resisted or ignored due to inter-agency rivalries.

If the strategy is a partnership of government, business and other non-governmental bodies, the location may be outside government. If so, there should still be a strong and direct link to the cabinet or its equivalent to maintain the commitment to, and influence of, the strategy.

The steering committee and secretariat may be set up for an indefinite or a specified time period. Since strategy development is unpredictable, it is important to allow for flexibility and for changes in the composition of the steering committee and secretariat as the strategy progresses. It is also important to ensure their continuity between phases or cycles of the strategy.

The steering committee and mandating authority

The function of the steering committee is to provide overall direction for the strategy, taking its mandate from the country's highest possible authority. It will also:

- facilitate inter-sectoral cooperation;
- ensure full participation and good coverage of the issues;
- consider the policy implications and refine the policy recommendations of the strategy; and
- keep the mandating authority and the participants informed at critical stages.

The mandating authority is the body that authorizes the steering committee to develop the strategy. It may be the chief executive of government, the cabinet, or the legislature. NEAPs usually call for a cabinet committee, specifically-formed for the purpose, to be chaired by the head of government. This disbands upon completion of the plan, which, in Africa, has usually taken about 18 months. The cabinet committee is asked to:

- provide policy direction;
- exercise ultimate authority for coordination;
- assure full government participation in the NEAP process;
- ensure that the cabinet is briefed on NEAP progress; and
- provide high-level back-up for the NEAP steering committee.

During the initial development of the strategy, and probably during its early implementation, it will be necessary for the steering committee to have clear authority for making decisions based on the outputs of the strategy (up to an agreed limit). But as the strategy engages more participants, and as it progresses from cycle to cycle, the character and function of the steering committee can be expected to change: it is likely to become less a coordinating and facilitating body and more a monitoring body.

Given this role, the steering committee should consist of high-level representatives of the main participants in the strategy. As the scope and nature of the strategy changes – and particularly if the participants change – the composition of the steering committee will probably have to change as well. In some countries, committee status may be considered inadequate. It could, therefore, have the status of a parastatal or permanent commission, reporting directly to cabinet. The Australian Resource Assessment Commission was a statutory authority established in 1989 to pursue the objectives of the National Ecologically Sustainable Development Strategy. Although abolished four years later, it provides a useful model for permanently institutionalizing a participatory strategy process at national level and is discussed further in Chapter 8.

The steering committee is likely to function best if it is chaired by an individual or institution acceptable to both the mandating authority and the main participants. The chairperson will be more effective if he or she is clearly impartial and independent of sectoral interests, and has strong vision and commitment to the strategy process.

The strategy secretariat

The strategy secretariat's function is to service the needs of the steering committee, and undertake the day-to-day organization and management of the strategy process. It will usually be responsible for the following:

- Facilitating and supporting participation. This could include coordinating nominated link officers from each of the main ministries and other participating groups. It would also include coordinating programmes and helping to develop the means for the active involvement of NGOs, communities and the business sector in all stages of the strategy.
- Assembling and analyzing information, at least during the main preparation phase of the strategy and whenever it is being reviewed.
- Assisting in policy drafting on behalf of participants, particularly cross-sectoral policy (line policies will usually be formulated by the responsible agencies).
- Assisting in action planning, particularly where a high degree of coordination is necessary or where there is no clear sectoral responsibility (usually most action planning will be done by the agencies and level of government concerned).

- Identifying those areas where capacity-building is most needed, and providing a training ground for developing capacities in process management and strategy preparation and implementation. This may involve initiating specific implementation programmes with relevant agencies within or outside government, and continuing support until capacities are adequate.
- Mounting demonstration programmes and projects in collaboration with relevant sectoral agencies and communities to build capacity, develop policy and guide implementation. These may take the form of demonstration strategies at local levels or focus on particular cross-sectoral themes such as biodiversity.
- Organizing and operating a communication programme, including preparing, revising and publishing strategy documents, keeping the steering committee and strategy participants informed of progress, providing public information and maintaining media relations, and editing reports and studies.
- Coordinating (at least initially) strategy implementation and monitoring.

The secretariat should be independent and have a well-defined authority in executing its tasks, reporting in most cases to the steering committee. It will need sufficient resources for its work (constantly searching for funds is debilitating for a strategy secretariat), including high quality staff.

The secretariat will need to be headed by someone with a good understanding of the strategy process, and of high standing in environment and/or development policy. He or she should command the respect of government, business and NGOs and have access to the highest levels while remaining open to all other levels. Depending upon the scope of the strategy, other professional staff would ordinarily cover economics; environmental and natural resource management; environmental impact assessment; social sciences; development and business; legislation and institutions; participation; communications, information and education. Administrative staff will also be required, including someone proficient in organizing seminars and workshops.

Continuity of secretariat staff is particularly important. Some secretariats have relied heavily on regular input by consultants to undertake various studies or activities. Although consultants have a crucial role, particularly in the flexibility they bring to the strategy process, there are substantial benefits in the secretariat having solid technical expertise within its own staff.

These benefits are enhanced if some secretariat staff are on secondment from key government agencies or NGOs. Long-term staffing arrangements:

- increase the usefulness of the strategy secretariat as a training ground for expertise in maintaining and institutionalizing the process;
- generate greater understanding and commitment to the process among the core staff;
- facilitate an integrated team approach in addressing many of the cross-sectoral issues;
- encourage a consistency in approach, momentum and continuity to the process;
- nurture links among the many participating groups; and
- ensure that the capacity is built up for quality control, particularly in information analysis, policy formulation and demonstration activities.

The secretariat need not be large if the expertise is permanently accessible within government, as is the case in Ethiopia. There, the secretariat comprises only three professionals but has continuing access to a wide network of government experts committed to the process through a system of committees (see Box 14). The main point is to not rely too heavily on the use of short-term consultants. Otherwise, written reports can dominate to the detriment of other elements of the process.

Participation and communications are driving forces interwoven with all aspects of strategy management. Their importance in national strategies has rarely been reflected in secretariat staff expertise. Team members need to have skills and experience in participation methods, social survey, conflict

Box 14: Staff resources in national strategy secretariats

The size of a strategy secretariat will depend on the maturity of the process (ie whether it has gone beyond its first cycle), its coverage and the extent to which the secretariat has been given responsibility for managing capacity-building and demonstration projects. The following examples illustrate the approach taken by a number of countries in Asia and Africa to staffing their strategy secretariats.

Bangladesh NCS: An expatriate adviser had the overall responsibility for the day-to-day running of the NCS secretariat, reporting to the executive vice-chairperson of the Bangladesh Agricultural Research Council, where the project was housed. Initial moves to establish the secretariat began in 1989, but it took more than a year to reach its full complement, which comprised the expatriate adviser, a national consultant, two junior technical officers and three support staff. The secretariat commissioned 20 background papers by selected national consultants and reviewers. The secretariat was disbanded in 1993 following completion of the NCS document.

Ethiopia NCS: From 1990 to 1994, the Ethiopian NCS secretariat was located in the Ministry of Planning and Economic Development. The secretariat was staffed by an Ethiopian NCS Director, with support from an Ethiopian professional, an expatriate adviser provided by IUCN, and two support staff. The secretariat worked through 29 regional task forces and 12 task forces at national level covering sectoral and inter-sectoral issues. For the implementation phase, beginning in late 1994, the secretariat is expected to be included in the structure of the new Ministry for Environment.

Guinea NEAP: An inter-ministerial unit was created in 1989 to take respon-sibility for the NEAP. Composed of seven civil servants, the unit was run on a day-to-day basis by the Secretary General of the Ministry of Planning and International Cooperation. He was supported by an expatriate technical adviser. The Guinean technical staff were not seconded full-time from their respective agencies. A further 80 civil servants were placed on monthly retainers to form 11 working groups for the preparation of thematic papers. This arrangement was changed in 1990 when the size of the groups was halved and a system of honoraria introduced for specific products. A core of regular short-term consultants was also used. The unit was disbanded in 1991.

Nepal NCS: At the height of activity during the NCS formulation phase (1985–88), the NCS secretariat comprised four technical experts, including an IUCN expatriate adviser, and four support staff. The NCS implementation programme secretariat, which began work in 1989, was built up in 1991 to 25 Nepalese technical staff, most

box continues

with expertise in ecology, environmental management and environmental engineering, plus 20 support staff. The NCS programme director also heads the Environment Division within the National Planning Commission. He is supported by one IUCN expatriate adviser.

Pakistan NCS: An NCS secretariat was established in 1988 and housed in the Environment and Urban Affairs Division (EUAD) to manage the process leading to the preparation of an NCS document. IUCN, which was commissioned by the government of Pakistan to develop the NCS, hired a Canadian and a Pakistani as joint coordinators of the secretariat. Various other expatriate and Pakistani expert staff worked with the secretariat for extended periods in the drafting process. In addition, 18 experts, along with three or four peer reviewers were commissioned to prepare various background papers. The NCS secretariat was disbanded on completion of the strategy document in 1991. An NCS unit was set up in the EUAD 18 months later and IUCN continues to maintain an NCS support unit. The NCS unit is being significantly upgraded to coordinate implementation activities.

Uganda NEAP: The NEAP secretariat, established in 1991, includes 12 government officials, 12 academics and 2 members from the private sector, in addition to the regular use of Ugandan consultants. Initially some 70 Ugandan experts working in nine sectoral task forces were commissioned to prepare background papers and undertake the necessary consultations. In 1992, these task forces were reduced in size to some three members each. In 1992, three technical expatriate advisers joined the secretariat which works within the Environment Department of the Ministry of Water, Energy, Minerals, and Environmental Protection.

---

resolution and group dynamics. Most countries have a richer experience in these fields through local strategies, which the strategy secretariat should seek to draw upon.

Organizing strategy start-up

An important distinction between the NCS and NEAP processes relates to the start-up phase. The NEAP sequence is usually as follows:

- initial missions of the World Bank lead to a decision by government to prepare an NEAP;
- through subsequent missions an agreement is drawn up among the Bank, the government and any other donors which may have become involved (ie UNDP, in the Zambian NEAP) which sets out the goals of the NEAP project, its outputs and activities including the institutional arrangements for undertaking them.

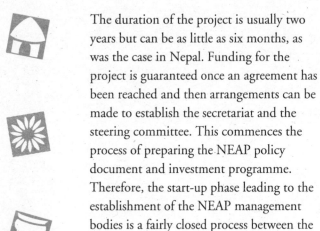

The duration of the project is usually two years but can be as little as six months, as was the case in Nepal. Funding for the project is guaranteed once an agreement has been reached and then arrangements can be made to establish the secretariat and the steering committee. This commences the process of preparing the NEAP policy document and investment programme. Therefore, the start-up phase leading to the establishment of the NEAP management bodies is a fairly closed process between the donors and government and includes commitment of funding for the full plan preparation process.

NCSs make more of the start-up phase: it is regarded as a key opportunity to increase participants' involvement in defining the approach to the strategy process. An initial agreement between the government and a technical support organization, usually IUCN, has been limited to the preparation of a project proposal, or what has sometimes been called an NCS prospectus. The steering committee and the secretariat are established for that purpose. A commitment to funding has normally covered only this initial phase, which seldom extends beyond a year and may involve as little as six months. On the basis of feedback from this document, the government then decides on the most appropriate way to move forward into the main strategy process. Continuity in funding has been a problem at this point; often because less attention has been given to nurturing donor involvement in the start-up phase than has been the case with the NEAP process.

If a government decides that an NSDS or other multi-sectoral national strategy is feasible, an early task will be to establish the steering committee and secretariat. The focus of their initial meetings, involving wider groups of participants where necessary, will be:

- defining the scope of the strategy and the main issues it should address;
- agreeing on, and prepare a statement concerning, the main purpose of the strategy and the expected outputs;
- reviewing previous or existing strategic processes, in the country and elsewhere, which may provide insight into designing the strategy process, or which could be used as vehicles for the strategy process (for example, the national and local planning systems, traditional decision-making structures) and reviewing other activities on which the strategy might build;
- identifying any critical capacity-building and training needs; and
- preparing a work plan and schedule of responsibilities including, in particular, a participation and communication plan.

On the basis of these initial discussions, the steering committee and secretariat should prepare the strategy proposal or prospectus. The main purpose of the prospectus is to help create an early understanding of the strategy and support for it. The participatory nature of the strategy can best be demonstrated and prepared for by allowing the prospectus to be worked on by a wide range of key potential participants for future phases of the process. Thoughtful participatory design at this stage may take more time but it is likely to save time later. In Pakistan, Nepal, Zambia, Canada and many other countries, the strategy proposal was widely circulated and formed the basis of public meetings and debate.

The strategy proposal or prospectus needs to cover:

- the main purpose of the strategy;
- the justification for undertaking the strategy;
- the means of building upon and integrating existing strategy processes;
- the issues to be covered;
- potential participants;
- an outline participation and communication plan;
- possible main steps in developing the strategy;
- ways to manage the process;
- expected outcomes and benefits of the strategy process;
- an outline work plan; and
- the resources required for the process.

If the government has not set aside the necessary resources for long-term support of the strategy programme and if donors have not yet made a commitment to support

anything beyond the start-up phase, then a key concern of the steering committee and secretariat during preparation of the strategy proposal will be to identify and make initial arrangements for the financing of future phases. In this respect, the prospectus should be reviewed as a funding proposal.

Start-up will need to be handled both diplomatically (to allay unnecessary fears about encroaching on rights and responsibilities) and with authority (to ensure that contributors treat the exercise with the attention that it deserves). The steering committee (and especially its chairperson) will need to be most active here. High-level seminars will be required to promote and explain the purpose of the strategy, and its likely benefits and implications. The seminars might involve the cabinet, permanent secretaries, the legislative body, and leaders of major sectors outside government. They would aim to secure the required high-level and multi-interest support for the strategy, and would continue at various stages throughout the process.

Conclusion

Managing strategies requires a broad combination of skills. In the past, an emphasis has been placed on technical skills in those fields which are the substantive focus of the process. Access to such technical expertise is vital for the central structures in strategy management, the steering committee and secretariat. But strategy experience has shown that the wide range of inter-personal skills that establish and maintain the 'circuitry' for powering the strategy are more important to managing the process.

A number of strategy principles govern the management approach and skills required:

- Strategy processes should mediate and build consensus among conflicting interests in resource use and, in so doing, seek equitable outcomes.
- Strategies should provide for the coordination and integration of effort between communities, between sectors and between levels of government by cutting across conventional boundaries in society.
- This will require that strategies be flexible and adaptive to changing circumstances; be innovative and opportunistic in taking advantage of new approaches or support structures; and, finally, retain the capacity for learning and reflection.

Most of these principles are concerned with people's inter-actions with one another, their sense of efficacy and of control over the forces which shape their environment. They concern the way decisions are made and the commitment a strategy team can engender among key participants to the process, from the most senior politicians to the diversity of small community groups. Strategies for sustainable development require new forms of management that can respond to these principles and demands.

Another key determinant of strategy management requires an understanding from the outset that the processes are permanent. They are not one-time events but part of a cyclical process of planning and action, which enables lessons learned from defining and implementing the strategy to feed into refining, amending and improving it as circumstances and situations change. In this sense, strategies for sustainable development are best viewed as processes for managing change. Effective strategies rely on adaptive management. Many outcomes will be uncertain as individual preferences, social norms, ecological conditions, technological capabilities, and the state of development change over time.

Strategies are highly political processes that continue in times when governments are hard pressed and are susceptible to short-term pressures of all sorts. Managing strategies requires thinking strategically. Strategy teams need to take a long-term perspective, but there is little point in doing so if many of the most powerful participants pull out of the process because it has departed from day-to-day realities. As one of IUCN's strategy network members in Latin America said at a recent network meeting:

'Having a strategy is like playing chess, but not having a strategy is like rolling dice.'

Avecita Chicchón,
Conservation International, Peru

Chapter 7

Planning the Strategy

A strategy is more likely to be successfully implemented if it concentrates on a few priority issues. These issues should be central to maintaining or improving the well-being of people and ecosystems and to achieving agreed economic objectives. They should be sufficiently high profile or be able to be tackled effectively to generate political support for the strategy. And the strategy should be able to make a clear difference in the way the existing decision-making system deals with the issues.

A few broad but well-defined and measurable objectives are necessary for each issue, to enable monitoring and evaluation of the strategy and ensure it gets results. Participants analyze the issues to reach agreement on the objectives, and the policies and actions required to achieve them. This includes preparing a policy framework as well as specific cross-sectoral and sectoral policies. The policy framework should clearly relate the strategy policy to the other policies of government (and of other participants in the strategy), identifying which policies may override it and the circumstances when they may do so, and which policies are subordinate. The last of the basic elements in planning a strategy is clearly defining the actions needed to put the policies into effect.

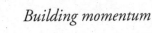

Building momentum

The start-up phase discussed in Chapter 6 should have left the strategy team with a number of strong assets to begin in earnest their work on strategy design. The basic management structure should be in place, with the steering committee and secretariat fulfilling their respective roles and answering to an authority, possibly a cabinet committee. This structure should have firm political backing and credibility among the key participants. Core funding, adequate for three to five years, should have been identified and a firm inter-active relationship established with any donors involved, including, even at this early stage, a mechanism for donor coordination. The setting should have been reviewed thoroughly for the potential to build on past or current strategies and to forge close working relations with those that have ongoing activities or structures which could reinforce the NSDS process. Finally, a range of initial thoughts should have been written down and discussed in sufficient detail for the decisions to be made to progress to a fully fledged strategy process. This documentation may have included a project proposal or prospectus which made an early attempt, with limited external input, to define the issues, purpose and strategy process.

The strategy team will now be in a position to enlarge the process into a broader range of interlocking activities. This chapter is about the planning or design of a strategy, from the definition of policy through to action planning. Yet it is particularly important at this point to begin implementation in fields which have already been defined and endorsed by government, possibly through other strategy processes. For example, if an NCS, TFAP, NEAP or Biodiversity Action Plan has established a framework for action for particular policies that would fall within the broader scope of an NSDS, then the strategy team should work with the appropriate agencies in nurturing their selective implementation.

It might be that the government has decided to retain and expand an existing strategy process, such as an NCS, which has come the full cycle and requires thorough policy review and revision. In that case, an implementation programme would be underway and would feed the updating process. The earlier that implementation begins, the better. This message is repeated often in this handbook and spelled out in Chapter 8.

How the detailed planning for a strategy proceeds will have a considerable influence on the level of commitment that the many interest groups or 'stakeholders' are likely to bring to implementation.

Five elements to planning a strategy

Strategies may be designed in a variety of ways but there are five generic elements which reflect the lessons of experience:

1. Choose the issues.
2. Analyse the issues.
3. Decide the objectives.
4. Draw together the policy framework.
5. Plan actions to implement the policies.

1. Choose the issues

Long preparation efforts can exhaust participants and produce policies and plans that are overtaken by events as soon as (or sometimes before) they are adopted. Preparation should be in proportion to what can be implemented. It is important to target only a few issues, within a coherent strategic framework, and approach them successfully.

It is axiomatic that a strategy is selective. The most comprehensive development strategies pay little attention to biodiversity or ecological processes. And the most ambitious conservation strategies devote much more time to environment and resources than to health or social issues. Even so, many multi-sectoral strategies have started out trying to cover more than is practical. Usually, their scope has narrowed sharply once their policies have been adopted and their implementation is due. The Pakistan NCS, for example, reduced its core programmes from 14 to 8, which still may be too many for the resources available.

The Netherlands began by limiting the scope of its National Environmental Policy Plan to eight themes, consisting of inter-connected issues with common environmental or economic causes (Box 15). The issues are crucial elements of the environment/ development problems faced by the Netherlands, and are few enough to be manageable.

Strategies that do not deliberately limit their scope waste time, money and effort on subjects they will end up doing little about. At best, this delays the point when the strategy tackles the priority issues. At worst, it increases the risk of the strategy losing political support and being dismissed as an unrealistic document.

Concentration on a few priority issues helps forge a unity of purpose among participants, gives focus to the strategy, and prevents it from becoming bogged down by trying to be too comprehensive. It is also easier to monitor and evaluate the strategy, and hence to keep it on track and ensure results.

The steering committee could help participants to reach agreement on priority issues by adopting criteria for deciding priorities. A priority issue might be one that meets the following criteria:

- It is central to sustainable development – to improving or maintaining human well-being and ecosystem well-being.
- Addressing it would build and maintain political support for the process. This may be because:

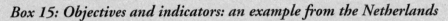

Box 15: Objectives and indicators: an example from the Netherlands

The ambitious goal of the Netherlands' National Environmental Policy Plan (NEPP) is to achieve sustainable development within one generation. The NEPP does not address the well-being of people and ecosystems directly but focuses instead on selected people–ecosystem interactions or 'themes' and the 'target groups' or sectors that are involved most directly in the interactions.

The themes are: climate change; depletion of the ozone layer; acidification; eutrophication; disposal of solid wastes; disturbance of local environments; dehydration of soils; and squandering of resources. Indicators have been devised for all the themes except the last two (due to a lack of data).

The target groups are: agricultural producers; the transport sector; chemical manufacturers; gas and electricity suppliers; the construction industry; consumers and retailers; the environmental protection industry; research and educational establishments; and environmental organizations, trade unions and voluntary bodies.

Each group is led by a steering committee, consisting of representatives of government and of the target group. The process is one of intensive networking and mediation. Participants set objectives and targets for their group; agree on actions to meet the targets; and have signed (or will sign) agreements with government, committing the group to the targets and actions.

Indicators play a crucial role in the NEPP, providing the means for setting targets and a measure of performance in meeting specific objectives. They have become a powerful strategic tool, used to define the contributions of each sector to an environmental problem, and hence to set both overall targets and targets for each sector.

— the issue is high on the political agenda (for whatever reason);
— the issue is already seriously affecting people, ecosystems, or both, over a significant proportion of the country, or will do so shortly if action is not taken; or
— it is highly probable that action on the issue will bring beneficial results soon.

• There is a clear niche in the decision-making system to address it. This niche may exist because:
— insufficient attention is being paid to human aspects (for example, the economic, social, cultural and other elements of an 'environmental' issue) or to ecosystem aspects (of a 'development'

issue) and there are opportunities to demonstrate the importance of addressing all aspects;
— addressing the issue would provide motivation and opportunity for removing obstacles to sustainable development that are embedded in society;
— the issue is being neglected; or
— a number of groups are tackling the issue but coordination and a more systematic approach would significantly improve their effectiveness.

The use of these three sets of criteria together enables the issue analysis and policy development to retain their strategic focus, while being pragmatic and opportunistic. For example, the inclusion of issues that are high on the political agenda, as well as issues that will bring quick benefits, is essential in maintaining and building political support for the process.

Assembling information

Choosing and analyzing the priority issues could begin with the circulation of a discussion paper suggesting the key sustainability issues facing the country. Depending on the approach taken during strategy start-up, the prospectus document or project proposal might serve this purpose, or at least provide the basic information for the discussion paper. This could be prepared as one of the first tasks of the secretariat in the planning phase. The aim is for the secretariat to prepare and circulate sufficient documentation to provide an agenda for informed discussion.

The manner in which the secretariat will facilitate wide participation from this point will vary according to different political and social circumstances. A common approach is the establishment of task forces. In the NEAP model, for example, the basic preparation of the plan is carried out by task forces, each focusing on a particular major environmental issue or group of issues. In the more successful NEAPs, such as Uganda's, and recently Zambia's, the task forces undertook visits to local communities, and conducted provincial or district workshops.

NCSs have also used task forces of various forms. In Ethiopia, 26 regional task forces, reflecting the administrative divisions at the time, and 11 sectoral and cross-sectoral task forces, were each assisted by the secretariat to conduct consultations and prepare their individual reports covering issues through to prescribed actions.

Any initial paper or set of papers prepared by the secretariat to simulate discussion needs to present the issues simply but not simplistically. The analysis should give different points of view – expert and non-expert – without taking sides on what are bound to be contentious matters. The purpose of these initial discussion papers is to:

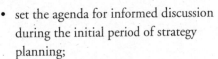

- set the agenda for informed discussion during the initial period of strategy planning;
- increase understanding of the complexity and dimensions of the issues and their inter-sectoral implications; and
- provide a focal activity around which the participatory process can be built.

Depending on the circumstances, information can be assembled by the secretariat and consultants in a wide variety of forms, including background studies, discussion papers, and audio-visual materials for use in a range of circumstances. The detailed communications and participation plans, which need to be prepared by the secretariat at this stage, will determine the forms in which this initial information is presented. The information can be obtained from:

- issue-based or regional task forces and associated workshops and meetings;
- government agencies (for example, they may be asked to prepare background papers, or provide published or unpublished statistics, a digest of material on file, consultation with an in-house expert, or the advice of a district office);
- short-term studies by academics or private consultants;
- short-term studies by strategy secretariat staff;
- a participatory inquiry or survey;
- longer-term research projects (to be undertaken as part of strategy implementation); and

- papers solicited from interest groups (NGOs, CBOs, etc.).

Terms of reference for studies will normally be prepared by the secretariat on the advice of the task forces. They will need to indicate the level of information required and the detail expected. It is important that background studies and discussion papers are not seen as 'chapters' of a strategy document; their role is to provide information and options for policy development.

Much of the information assembly, analysis and preparation of policy options should be undertaken by the government agencies responsible for the resources or sector concerned. This will enable use to be made of the expertise and information base of these agencies. It will also provide the agencies with opportunities to consider their responsibilities from a broader perspective than usual, taking account of their cross-sectoral and longer-term implications. Universities, research and policy institutions and independent professionals also have important contributions to make, particularly on issues that require independent analysis or subjects that are outside the expertise or mandates of particular agencies.

During the development of the Pakistan NCS, background studies were prepared by inter-disciplinary working groups, including a writing team, sectoral and other agencies concerned, experts from academia, and others. This overcame a problem common to many strategy processes: the difficulty of finding sectoral experts with a good grasp of the cross-sectoral approach.

Another method is to organize a series of workshops to generate the material required. A strategy secretariat member or consultant would then finalize materials for subsequent review by workshop participants and others.

There is no single best way of going about this early information gathering, choosing the priority issues and widening the network of participants. Yet the steering committee and secretariat, as part of their work pro-gramme, will need to clearly spell out the approach they settle on and communicate it widely. Efficient management and coordi-nation will lend credibility to the process as it gains momentum.

2. Analyse the issues

Issue analysis has two important functions:

- revealing what changes the strategy should aim to generate with respect to the priority issues, and how it should do so; and
- providing a reason and an opportunity for participants to work together, to recognize common problems and to devise mutually acceptable solutions.

Issue analysis, or problem definition, is intimately related to developing participa-tion. If interest groups agree on what the

problem is, they are halfway to a solution. Issue analysis gives participants something tangible to work with and a reason for involvement. As learning takes place, the analysis can be revised a number of times if necessary.

Issue analysis should challenge the interest groups by including forecasts of likely devel-opments in the absence of policy (or if current policies remain unchanged). For example, what are the implications for Asian societies of the 300 million cars that automobile manufactures forecast Asians will buy in the next 30 years? Participants should consider:

- the impacts of current policies;
- new policies or policy changes that are needed; and
- likely impacts of the new policies, including costs and benefits.

Developing different scenarios is a useful way of exploring these impacts. For example, one scenario could portray the likely results if current policies remain unchanged. Two other scenarios could explore the likely costs and benefits of alternative policies; one meeting targets quickly, the other more gradually.

Analysis will need to:

- identify which issues are common across the sectors and interest groups, and which are more specific;

Box 16: *Suggested components of analysis*

Trends in resources and ecosystems: their quantity, quality, use, ownership and management; ecological limits to resource use (within which sustainable social and economic activity must operate) under given technologies.

Identification of **policy and economic forces** that underlie resource/ecosystem use in major sectors and population groups. These will be both international and national; for example, debt, trade, structural adjustment, exchange rates, taxation and pricing policy, government income and expenditure, balance of payments and employment.

Identification of the **responses of different sectors** and population groups to these policy and economic forces.

Assessment of the **importance and relevance of the resource base** and ecosystems for different groups of the population, analysing the relationships between the environment/resource base and demographic characteristics, incomes, health and welfare.

Detailed sectoral analyses of forestry, agriculture, human settlements, fisheries, energy, transport, industry and tourism, etc. These would examine the types and rates of use of resources/ecosystems by each sector, with respect to sector growth and productivity. In addition, they would analyse how sectors treat the links between economic, social and environmental subsystems: what are the sectoral objectives for each subsystem, how are trade-offs made in achieving these objectives, and what are their impacts?

Cross-sectoral analyses examining the interactions among major sectors. These would analyse the impacts of one sector on another; for example, resource flows, and physical, public health and landscape impacts. They would look at cross-sectoral integration in institutional, legal and planning issues: where are there gaps, conflicts, compatibilities and synergies?

Provisional assessment of the sustainability of resource/ecosystem use by each major economic sector or population group: covering effects on biodiversity, ecological processes, natural capital stocks and the sustainability of yields, economic viability, and social welfare and equity. For most issues, however, it is unlikely that there will be adequate information (time series) to make definitive statements about sustainability.

Analysis of the principal functional/institutional constraints to sustainability in terms of policy, planning processes, institutional roles and capacities, legislation, education and awareness, training, technologies, financial allocations and procedures,

box continues

capacities to monitor the development process, etc. Where are there overlaps, gaps and conflicts? Where are coordination and capacity-building required?

Analysis of development and environment patterns and consequences with respect to ethical considerations and national goals.

Definition of priority issues — problems and opportunities — to be resolved by the strategy.

Development of different scenarios and options with costs and benefits of each.

Outline policy recommendations, from above analyses.

- identify the key influences on the issues, and the most effective ways of dealing with them;
- study any action already being taken;
- agree on which issues are negotiable in the short-term and which cannot be resolved until later; and
- agree on the most efficient policy provisions and other actions to address the priority issues.

It is useful to analyse the issue sectorally and cross-sectorally. The former enables the role and impact of each sector to be clearly defined and allows policy proposals to be closely related to existing sectoral mandates. The latter breaks down sectoral barriers and helps participants to think strategically.

A sector analysis examines each sector and its contribution to development and environment, and then looks at cross-sectoral issues to identify possible conflicts and compatibilities among sectors. This is likely to be closer to the forms of analysis with which planners are familiar. More important, it is easy to relate to – and therefore to influence – the existing policy-making system. It also, however, runs the risk of repeating the usual sectoral plans and failing to provide much new insight. In addition, sector-focused analysis is very time-consuming, and can produce large amounts of information that may not be useful for the strategy. It can also tend to treat some key issues superficially.

A cross-sectoral or thematic analysis identifies a set of major problems and opportunities facing the country, and then examines their sectoral and cross-sectoral roots. That approach was adopted by the Dutch for their National Environmental Policy Plan (see Box 15). This enables participants to think strategically from the start and ensures that time and money are not wasted by collecting and analysing information that will not be used. Although a process of analysis which crosses sectoral boundaries is often contentious and meets

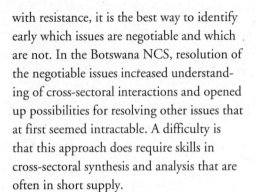

with resistance, it is the best way to identify early which issues are negotiable and which are not. In the Botswana NCS, resolution of the negotiable issues increased understanding of cross-sectoral interactions and opened up possibilities for resolving other issues that at first seemed intractable. A difficulty is that this approach does require skills in cross-sectoral synthesis and analysis that are often in short supply.

The initial information gathering, through to defining the priority issues and the consideration of different scenarios, will involve a number of stages and components in the strategy's approach to the analysis of information. Components of this process of analysis are suggested in Box 16.

The steering committee and secretariat will need to determine who undertakes the various components of analytical work. In some strategies, the sectoral and cross-sectoral analysis has been done by special task forces while other components are undertaken by government agencies, consultants, NGO participants, or the secretariat. Problems of information overload are common in strategies; systems will need to be set in place so that information is readily accessible and able to be manipulated (Box 17).

3. Decide the objectives

'If you don't know where you are going, any road will get you there.'

The scope of sustainable development may be too broad to be encompassed by a single strategy. Therefore, strategies might progress best by focusing on achieving a few specific objectives. For example, a local strategy for the Sierra Nevada de Santa Marta in Colombia and the Dutch National Environmental Policy Plan both have the ultimate goal of sustainable development, but their specific objectives are more limited. The Santa Marta strategy focuses on improving and maintaining the quality and flow of water. The Dutch strategy concentrates on reducing pollution.

Objectives are at the heart of the strategy. This means they will not all be agreed to at once. Preliminary objectives may be proposed early on for the sake of discussion, but the objectives agreed to toward the end of issue analysis are likely to be significantly different from those advanced at the beginning. For this reason, it is somewhat misleading to speak of objective-setting and issue analysis as separate steps. They go together.

Objectives are needed for each issue. They should be:

- few enough to be achievable;
- broad enough to ensure the support of participants and encompass all aspects of the issue; and
- narrow enough and clearly defined enough to be measurable.

Box 17: A sustainable development information system

The more comprehensive the strategy, the greater the information it requires and generates, and the more challenging the information management problem. It may be worth considering establishing a Sustainable Development Information System as an integral part of the strategy process. This could consist of either a central office with, for example, hard-copy and computer files of information, plus maps and air photos, or a network of existing data centres with an agreement and procedures for cooperation on the strategy.

Individual countries may also find it helpful to identify and maintain registers (preferably computer-based) of their national expertise base — institutions and individuals in the government and non-governmental sectors with experience and skills relevant to sustainable development. This resource will be required to play a central role in providing technical and resource information and leading debate in the strategy process, and also in implementing, monitoring and evaluating the strategy.

While many countries do not yet have such registers, most bilateral donors, multilateral development banks and consultancy companies maintain rosters of environmental and sustainable development expertise, both individual and institutional. Independent, publicly-accessible registers of individual professionals who have worked internationally are maintained by both IIED and IUCN on separate but identically structured and shared databases. Making such information available may be a significant role for outside organizations and agencies in the strategy process.

Objectives that meet these criteria are required to assess progress with the strategy. They are also essential for the strategy to make actual progress. They are the logical complement to concentrating on a few priority issues. They help the participants focus their efforts to understand the implications of the strategy. Objectives give participants a yardstick with which they can measure progress; hence, they can also give participants a sense of direction and, eventually, achievement.

Strategy objectives generally will fall into two categories: those that set a long-term vision for sustainable development (for example, 20 years or a generation), and those that are consistent with the long-term vision, but tailored to a shorter time, such as the project or development cycle.

As an illustration, the specific objectives set by the National Strategy for Ecologically Sustainable Development in Australia are presented in Box 18.

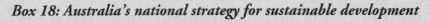

Box 18: Australia's national strategy for sustainable development

Australia prepared an NCS in 1983 following wide consultation within government and with the private sector. A unit within the ministry responsible for environment provided the secretariat. The NCS was a highly compromised document, reflecting the predominance of development interests in Australian politics at the time. Within government, for example, it was up to the environment agencies to prove unsustainability when considering major development proposals from other agencies. Through the 1980s the onus of proof shifted to the development agencies so that, where there was doubt about the possible consequences of an action, a decision should err on the side of caution.

It was in this changing climate that, in 1989, a national summit of industry, unions and conservation organizations was convened to begin defining principles of what, in Australia, is called Ecologically Sustainable Development (ESD). With this began the process of preparing a National Strategy for Ecologically Sustainable Development (NSESD). A number of ESD discussion and policy papers were released and nine working groups were established involving government, the private sector and NGOs in order to undertake strategy planning in the sectors of: agriculture, energy production, energy use, fisheries, forest use, manufacturing, mining, tourism and transport. A draft strategy was prepared on the basis of working group reports and released for public comment and a final NSESD was published late in 1992, ten years after the preparation of the NCS. The strategy has been adopted by the Australia's federal, state and territory governments.

The goal of the strategy is development that improves the total quality of life, both now and in the future, in a way that maintains the ecological processes on which life depends.

Core objectives are:

- to enhance individual and community well-being and welfare by following a path of economic development that safeguards the welfare of future generations;
- to provide for equity within and between generations; and
- to protect biological diversity and maintain essential ecological processes and life-support systems.

Guiding principles are:

- decision-making processes should effectively integrate both long- and short-term economic, environmental, social and equity considerations;

box continues

- where there are threats of serious or irreversible environmental damage, lack of full scientific certainty should not be used as a reason for postponing measures to prevent environmental degradation;
- the global dimension of environmental impacts of actions and policies should be recognized and considered:
- the need to develop a strong, growing and diversified economy which can enhance the capacity for environmental protection should be recognized;
- the need to maintain and enhance international competitiveness in an environmentally sound manner should be recognized;
- cost-effective and flexible policy instruments should be adopted, such as improved valuation, pricing and incentive mechanisms; and
- decisions and actions should provide for broad community involvement on issues which affect them.

These guiding principles and core objectives are considered as a package. No objective or principle predominates over any others.

It was easy for participants in the British Columbia Land Use Strategy to agree on principles for conserving ecological processes and biodiversity, but much more difficult to agree on objectives, such as the percentages of different types of forest to be protected in parks. Addressing such objectives forced participants to discuss the role of protected areas in sustainable development, and how much protection is enough and why. In due course, the discussions changed the consensus on this issue.

The policy framework

The results of the various analyses and debates on issues will need to be collated by the secretariat with help from the task forces. It will also be necessary to record where

consensus has and has not been achieved. Further work can then be done on the priority issues and objectives; the aim being to detail specific policy provisions, primarily addressing those issues and objectives where consensus has been reached.

Throughout the process, from the earliest stages of issue definition, various levels of policy will have been discussed and some will have been adopted as the favoured course of action by participants. The secretariat will need to draw these levels together within one framework so that the broad principles, goals, and objectives of the strategy (the broad policies) can provide the umbrella for more specific objectives and operational criteria, standards and targets (the specific policies).

It is important to move quickly from consideration of the broad policies to that of the more specific. As participants found during the development of the British Columbia Land Use Strategy, it is usually quite easy for participants to agree on generalities that give wide latitude for interpretation, masking crucial differences among competing interests. The Australian NCS document was too general in drawing policies on the most contentious issues. This allowed the mining industry to use the document to argue the case for large-scale exploitation of mineral resources in Kakadu National Park, a World Heritage Site. The Australian National Parks and Wildlife Service, which fought the mining industry in the high court on the issue, did not share this interpretation of the NCS policies. The policy framework should therefore set out a long-term vision of what is sustainable, together with medium- and short-term policies to move in that direction.

Focusing on specific objectives, standards and targets will bring out the real debate on sustainable development. The task of participants in the strategy is not to try to bring the debate on every issue to a quick resolution: debate on some issues is likely to continue for many years. Rather, the aim is to reach agreement on how to respond to some of the major problems and, in so doing, make progress towards sustainable development. Ultimately, some key issues for the strategy will need to be resolved by an arbitrating authority, usually the government. Institutional reforms such as the creation of the Resources Assessment Commission in Australia, can be set up to deal with these situations as part of the strategy process. Eventually, some issues may need to be resolved by parliament in the form of legislation. The secretariat always has the option of developing detailed policies, even where consensus has not been reached, with a view to these being settled through the strategy steering committee or in cabinet.

The framework should set out levels of policy that become progressively more focused. Specific policies relating to a priority objective would outline the reforms required to address it, covering:

- training, education and communications;
- legislation, regulations and standards;
- institutions;
- economic instruments and market-based policies;
- development programmes;
- planning systems and procedures;
- human and financial resources;
- technology innovation and research; and
- monitoring and evaluation systems.

Specific policies need to include clear guidance on their most appropriate practical interpretation. This practical expression may need to be demonstrated or tested through special demonstration projects or facilitating programmes as part of strategy implementation.

Relationship to other policies

The policy framework should clearly relate strategy policies to other policies of government (and of other partners in the strategy); defining which policies may override it and the circumstances under which they may do so, and which policies are subordinate. Sectoral policies within the scope of the strategy are likely to be subordinate to the strategy, for example. But the finance ministry's policy on annual budget plans may be overriding. If so, it will be important to review the budget plans' criteria for programmes and projects to ensure that activities called for by the strategy receive high priority.

The policy framework will also need to clearly define how it links with and builds upon other strategies operating at national or other levels of government. To avoid the strategy becoming marginalized and irrelevant, sectoral policy development and planning will have to be drawn into the process. This can be done by ensuring that the strategy has the proper authority, and by clearly defining at the outset its relationship with other decision-making processes. It is important that participants in all sectors understand which elements of their policy-making, planning and implementation will become, in effect, their sector's contribution to the strategy, and which elements will be left outside the scope of the strategy. Making agency policy development and planning an explicit part of the strategy will also help to integrate sectors.

Review and revision of policy framework

The strategy policy framework should be subject to periodic reviews, timed to take best advantage of the country's existing development cycles. Making and reviewing specific cross-sectoral and sectoral policies is a continuing part of the strategy process. Policy formulation, particularly cross-sectoral policies, should be widely participatory. The actual drafting of cross-sectoral policies may be done by the strategy secretariat, an inter-sectoral team, or a central agency. Usually, sectoral policy review and reform will continue to be done by the line agency concerned.

The policy framework will need also to define indicators so that progress towards the objectives and targets may be monitored and evaluated. Defining indicators can also help to make the objectives and targets more specific.

Action plans

An action plan should be part of a strategy's policy framework. Yet in work on strategies to date, it has been found convenient to separate out the broad policy framework from specific action prescriptions. The Nepal NCS document, for example, presents national and sectoral policies together, then revisits these in the form of a more detailed Conservation Action Agenda. There was a tendency in the early NCSs to emphasize building agreement on broad policy while leaving more detailed prescriptions to be taken up as the policies filtered through government and other sectors in society. Many of the early World Bank-initiated NEAPs, on the other hand, tended to leap straight to specific project prescriptions with little emphasis on broad-level consensus-building. Today the NEAP model usually includes the preparation, over a year, of an NEAP Policy Document and a separate Environmental Investment Programme. This was the case in the Zambian NEAP, initiated in 1993.

Many NCSs have also evolved to give more detailed expression to various forms of action plans. In Vietnam, the most recent document prepared in the NCS strategy process was a portfolio of project concepts, each with a simple budget. In a regionally coordinated programme that begin in 1992, South Pacific island countries are being assisted in preparing national environment management plans, which bind broad policy prescriptions and a project concept portfolio into one document for each country.

In the Ethiopia NCS, a national policy document – drawing from those policy documents previously defined by regional level government – took two years to prepare and was completed in early 1994. Detailed investment programmes are now being developed over the next year by the regional authorities and sectoral agencies to give more detailed expression to the policies.

The purpose of an action plan or investment programme is to enable implementation of the provisions of the overall policy framework. The plan needs to flesh out the policy prescriptions and define programmes and projects that directly address the priorities for action. There are several important principles to consider when deciding on the comprehensiveness and level of detail of an action plan:

- Keep well in mind the concept of a strategy for sustainable development as a continuing and iterative process in which the main components are repeated. It is not necessary to prescribe actions covering everything. The idea is to get going on priority problems for which results are achievable. An action plan should expand and deepen over time with reflection on experience.
- The people responsible for implementing the policies should be involved in preparing the action plan, as is the case with the Ethiopian NCS. Organizations which will be involved in arranging resources for implementation also need to be involved in action planning.
- The process of designing specific programmes and projects for priority attention should be complemented by the equally important task of reviewing and redefining existing development investment against the strategy's principles.

These points are taken up in more detail in the remaining chapters, but they should be borne in mind when considering the specific approaches suggested in this section.

Maintain government commitment to action plans

The secretariat should develop a cross-sectoral action plan which addresses the basic elements of an institutional framework for sustainable development: the capacities needed for these reforms to work, including the skills in various essential decision-making methods such as environmental assessment (EA); and a series of demonstration programmes and projects undertaken with line agencies which test the policy innovations proposed in the strategy. The line ministries will also need to carefully define their sectoral action plans; these might include a range of new initiatives where gaps have been identified and where new relationships and procedures need to be built, and necessary adjustments to existing programmes and projects.

By this stage in the strategy a strong network of government technical staff should have become fully engaged in the process. Desk officers, who will be responsible for carrying forward the actions, need to be the main creative force in detailing the plans. This would help to avoid a key problem of past strategies, where action plans may have involved consultation (as distinct from participation) but essentially have been prepared by consultants.

Attracting donor funding often requires that project concepts be developed into comprehensive proposals; it is at this point that busy government teams often lose their sense of ownership. An up-front commitment to a concept is very important but is rarely made by external funding agencies. Donors need to acquire a special sensitivity, flexibility and patience in making early commitments to support the necessarily slow process of negotiation and discussions that must accompany programme design within government.

Involve the private sector

Key participants in action planning should also include non-governmental actors, particularly the business sector. Industry's participation is essential, both as an implementer and as an investor, but it is, by far, one of the least tried and tested aspect of strategies. Industry representatives should be included in various round table discussion groups from the earliest stages. Targeted private sector action plans (these are common, for example, in the transport, energy or agricultural sectors) can then be negotiated to encourage or discourage selected activities. Often, government and the donor community will need to give special attention to nurturing private sector action planning. In Nepal, for example, industry, government and local communities have been involved in developing pollution action plans for 'hot spot' industrial areas.

Once the broad areas for action have been set with the private sector, then more focused action planning relating to specific areas can be a continuing process. A good deal of innovation and flexibility will need to be shown by government and donors in designing a range of instruments to support and encourage this process.

Processes of structural adjustment promoted by the World Bank and the International Monetary Fund (IMF) are often a powerful factor to be considered in defining action plans for the private sector in developing countries. Such international organizations are currently not oriented or equipped to approach the design of structural adjustment programmes as action plans for sustainable development. Narrow economic criteria predominate and, in order to reorient them, strategy teams will have to work closely with those involved in structural adjustment packages. In Nepal, IUCN helped the IMF determine the feasibility and cost of improving the environmental performance of the major tannery in the Kathmandu valley, so that these factors could be included in plans for structural adjustment.

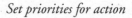

Set priorities for action

Over time in the strategy cycle there will be a need and an opportunity for subsidiary action plans and a need for a more complete expression of the original action points. This will take the pressure off the strategy team to cover everything from the outset. The secretariat needs to constantly keep in mind that the top priority issues must be addressed first. In fact, if agreement on a range of actions relating to a key issue is reached early in the strategy process, then the secretariat should feel free to seek endorsement for them there and then. There are great advantages to the action plan being adopted for implementation in these staged editions. It allows for the more straightforward actions to proceed, and builds momentum and confidence in the process. Also, past experience has shown that if an action plan is delivered as a single package, many of the more difficult, less defined and less attractive actions fall by the wayside.

There may be political pressure on the secretariat to come up with one action plan 'product'. The World Bank NEAP model, for example, requires this. A consolidated version, or at least a clear indication of how the various action plan elements relate to each other, can be produced. This is desirable, in any case, to ensure that the overall strategic framework for the package is appreciated.

Box 19: Changes likely to be covered by an action plan

Changes to development policies, national development plans, sectoral master plans, and regional plans, to ensure appropriate vertical integration as well as integration with environmental and social policies.

Integration of environmental and social considerations into programme and project cycles. Environmental assessment is one way of doing this.

Reforms to economic policies, resource allocation and property rights policies, and sectoral policies and practices for environmental protection, natural resource management and development.

Adoption of economic instruments and other policy tools to integrate economic, social and environmental objectives.

Changes to legislation. These may include new umbrella laws, amendments to existing laws to incorporate standards and practices to ensure sustainability, and changes to rules and regulations.

Institutional strengthening and organizational development. Institutional strengthening entails creating new or better-equipped political, economic and social institutions, and links between them, to address issues of sustainability directly; and establishing links between existing public service institutions. Organizational development entails amending the mandates, policy documents, objectives, corporate strategies, functions and programmes (internal management and administration as well as professional), organizational structures, staffing, funding sources, and protocols concerning external relations to promote sustainability.

Education and training to develop the necessary attitudes and skills.

Categories of action

Five categories of inter-related actions can be identified, relating to:

1. policy, legislative, institutional and organizational change (as in Box 19);
2. new cross-sectoral decision-making methods, such as environmental assessment, risk analysis and forecasting;
3. capacity-building that relates to the ability of organizations to make the new instruments and methods work;
4. specific new programmes and projects; and
5. a wide range of adjustments and innovations to existing programmes and investments.

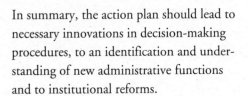

In summary, the action plan should lead to necessary innovations in decision-making procedures, to an identification and understanding of new administrative functions and to institutional reforms.

New laws, institutions or other major policy changes should not precede a full appreciation of the processes and functions they will fulfill. In some cases, the need for a new law or institution may be so well-recognized and enunciated in the endorsed policy framework that the government can act immediately. In most cases, although a policy commitment may be made, further effort will be required to bring on board those who will be involved in implementation. They can then appreciate the administrative implications, have a role in detailing the proposed reforms, and, most important, be able to raise their own capacity and commitment. Voluntary initiatives to implement the policy often may precede, and perhaps even obviate the need for, legislation.

For example, a government may make a commitment to establishing an effective national system of environmental assessment. Having a small local or international team prepare EA legislation for submission to cabinet and legislature is usually not the best way to ensure successful implementation. Instead, it may be more effective to develop a participatory programme in which technical people from key sectors are helped to prepare and field test EA procedures

suited to national conditions, which subsequently can be expressed in law (as necessary). This was the approach adopted in Nepal through the Environment Core Group. The action plan needs to define this kind of development programme for any policy, legislative, institutional or organizational change for which there is likely to be inadequate understanding, acceptance or capabilities for implementation.

In some cases, such as a new environment agency, there may be no ideal structure, merely principles that need to be followed in such matters as its status and independence. There are several models which could probably serve the purpose equally well. The strategy secretariat should provide cabinet with alternatives and a favoured option. The final decision will be a political one.

Each action needs to be clearly defined in terms of:

- its purpose, broadly covering what needs to be done over the strategy cycle;
- specified inputs and outputs to shorter term target dates;
- implementation arrangements;
- roles and responsibilities of each implementing agent;
- critical tasks and critical paths, including links to other projects and programmes;
- a budget and financial plan, identifying public investment requirements and priorities and other economic implications of the action plan (including

cost-benefit analysis); and

- monitoring and evaluation arrangements.

Relationship to development planning and assistance

The action plan should dovetail with the national, sectoral and subsidiary development planning processes. The action plan – or at least the components to be implemented by government – would normally have to be submitted for approval of the financial and resource implications. This is likely to be a separate process from approval of the policy framework.

The type of action plan and budget will vary widely among countries. Some elements of the action plan could be made the subject of a donors' conference. As the Pakistan NCS experience has shown, the strategy process as a whole has proved to be a promising vehicle for replacing conventional concepts of aid conditionality, moving from a situation in which conditions are set by donors, to one in which they are defined by the recipient country; or to an effective combination of both (Chapter 10). However, attracting aid should not be the main preoccupation of the strategy.

Planning for implementation must recognize the existing constraints of the government and (where relevant) donors. Current economic recessions and other constraints have made the possibility of obtaining substantial amounts of new development aid money very unlikely. If anything, aid budgets are getting smaller. Also, the governments of many lower-income countries are unable to absorb significant amounts of new money, due to limited institutional capacity to undertake development projects.

Therefore, a critical step in ensuring implementation of a strategy is to assess how the recommended programmes and actions fit within the current circumstances of governments and donors. This does not mean that the policy framework and action plan need be less creative in their vision. Rather, the action plan must spell out the steps to lead governments and donors to implementation. Funding constraints also point up the crucial need for business and industry to participate fully in the strategy.

Immediate short-term measures to refocus existing investments include adding an environmental assessment component to a programme or project to better determine effects and mitigative measures (using strategy criteria in the EA framework). Another way to try and turn the focus toward sustainability is adding an environmental management component to current projects that are likely to have negative environmental consequences.

The action planning process must also help national planning commissions (or similar agencies) sort out what to do immediately with the long shopping list of projects

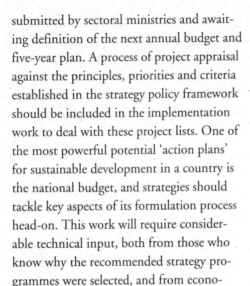

submitted by sectoral ministries and await-
ing definition of the next annual budget and
five-year plan. A process of project appraisal
against the principles, priorities and criteria
established in the strategy policy framework
should be included in the implementation
work to deal with these project lists. One of
the most powerful potential 'action plans'
for sustainable development in a country is
the national budget, and strategies should
tackle key aspects of its formulation process
head-on. This work will require considerable technical input, both from those who
know why the recommended strategy programmes were selected, and from econo-
mists familiar with planning budgets.

National planning bodies usually provide
the channel for reviewing government
programmes against national goals. They are
a good way to introduce the concerns of
sustainable development. Of course, the
goal is to have these concerns addressed well
before in the sectors themselves. Thus, when
programmes are delivered for coordinated
review against a broader strategic framework, it can be assumed that they are
internally consistent with sustainability
principles.

In developing countries, the sector programme review process within national
planning agencies is weak. It often amounts
to little more than assembling the various
sectoral programmes and passing them on to
finance agencies where the real decisions,
cuts and reallocations are made. Strategy

teams will need to identify the main
decision points, what is decided and how, in
the allocation of public resources. Exercises
can be designed to be undertaken within
national planning bodies which address
these issues and bring together the action
planning, implementation and capacity-
building elements of a strategy.

Two interesting exercises of this kind were
undertaken in Bhutan and Nepal as part of
national strategy processes. In Nepal, as a
step in developing a national system of EA,
some 30 members of the environment core
group drawn from the different sectors
worked within the National Planning
Commission (NPC) for a number of weeks.
They reviewed more than 40 projects
submitted as elements of the annual
programmes from sectoral ministries. Access
was given to all NPC files and budget
documents. The goal was to test various EA
procedures and criteria which the group had
defined in previous exercises and to identify
planning gaps and weakness in the projects
under review. Most important, the group
also defined the weaknesses in administrative procedures, capacities and structures
within the NPC and the various agencies to
which it related.

The review was in response to an action
defined by the original NCS Conservation
Action Agenda (ie that there should be an
EA system) but it also resulted in a wide
range of recommended actions that began to
address more fundamental difficulties.

In Bhutan, a similar but more restricted review was undertaken, by the National Environment Strategy Secretariat, of all projects which at the time were before the NPC. This exercise was not as effective because it was one-off and not undertaken as part of a broader participatory endeavour to develop EA procedures.

These examples show why the strategy process needs to be ongoing and iterative and why the various skills and mechanisms for review are so important (addressed as monitoring and evaluation in Chapter 9).

Conclusion

Most strategies, from the initial wave of NCSs in the early 1980s through to the diverse range of types now undertaken, have been viewed as one-time planning exercises. Many of the NCSs and several of the more recent NEAPs have been compiled through consultative mechanisms akin to those which evolved during the 1970s for the development of land-use plans. Many strategies are even called plans, such as those following the NEAP model: the National Environment Management Plans of the South Pacific Islands, the Green Plan in Canada, and the Dutch National Environment Policy Plan.

Even though most have been much more ambitious and interactive than their names imply, there has often been no vision for the process beyond final endorsement of the document. Implementation has been seen as crucial to the plan's success but as something apart. Secretariats have usually closed down once a plan has been prepared and the idea of returning to the planning phase to review and revise the policy framework and action plan has been absent. This critical reassessment process has been taken for granted in conventional development planning, but not in the case of early strategies. Most of them were born through conservation or environment imperatives and have gradually evolved to be more conscious of their leading role.

Strategies have to date been viewed as projects with a predetermined lifespan and end product. Some development planners believe this is how it should be and that to regard strategies as an ongoing process would undermine their impact in a world where political realities give governments and donors alike short-term time horizons and pressure to deliver. Strategies must respect and take advantage of these political realities but, if they are to determine the way development takes place, then they need to become an integral part of the machinery of government.

Another trend reflected in the strategy experience is that a country cannot have effective centralized planning and decentralized implementation. As the common principles for development reflected in most strategies begin to change the structures and ways decisions are made then, inevitably, the

nature of strategy planning will also change. Greater emphasis will need to be given to devolution in countries where the centralizing forces have failed to nurture the local level. Methods for linking national strategy planning with strategies developing at local level and across government sectors will become more important. The Ethiopian NCS process has made a good start in this respect. Now that strategies are underway in most provinces of Pakistan, the next phase of planning within the NCS will look very different than it did in the first round, however successful that may have been.

There are two main challenges, then, facing national strategy planning over the next decade. The first is to convince governments that strategies should been seen as continuous, cyclical processes, integrated into and changing conventional development cycles. The second is to help build strategies at sub-national levels and establish effective working links among strategies so that, in future, the detail of policies and action plans will be generated by the institutions and communities responsible for implementing them.

Chapter 8

Implementing the Strategy

The sooner implementation begins, the sooner a strategy can benefit from experience. Early action brings greater commitment and momentum to the process, in addition to developing essential management capacities. Other strategies for action throughout government and at local levels will be needed. These include implementation by government, the private sector and NGOs. Each has a key function, which can be helped through the appropriate legal frameworks, economic instruments and mechanisms for mediation and conflict resolution. There should be an emphasis on cooperation rather than compulsion.

The strategy secretariat or similar body has an important role to play, particularly through demonstration and pilot programmes bridging a number of sectors. Responsibility for implementation becomes more diffuse with each turn of the strategy cycle, and as the institutional mechanisms for sustainable development mature. These will include new forms of partnership that emphasize flexibility, informality and open approaches to problem-solving and consensus-building.

Implementation from day one

Strategies are cyclical processes, with capacity-building and implementation continuing throughout. Implementation feeds into, and is guided by, regular review and revision of the policy framework and action plan, based on monitoring and evaluation.

The layers of implementation – by different levels and sectors of government and by a wide range of actors outside government – are likely to deepen with each turn of the cycle. The strategy's policy and action plan benefit increasingly as plans turn to actions, and as lessons from these actions lead to better policy and greater capacity.

Implementation can begin from the earliest stage of a strategy, in fields where government or a group of other participants is already committed to action.

Nothing reinforces a strategy process more than actions beginning to take effect. As a general rule, the earlier and more directly participants can feel the impact of strategy actions, the more they will be committed to the process. This rule reflects three important lessons of strategy experience:

1. The groups involved, whether politicians or local communities, need to see the practical relevance and benefits of the strategy process as an incentive to participate. Early action in priority areas can satisfy this need while bringing a sense of ownership and understanding of the strategy process.

2. In situations of rapid change, policy development within a strategy can be overtaken by events unless it is also acting to shape them. When actions are taken, there are often winners and losers, and the strategy team will need to find ways of minimizing the negative burdens of change and innovation if pockets of resistance are not to develop. (This concern is discussed later with respect to private sector activities.)

3. Early action helps to build capacity.

There is no limit to the kinds of implementation that can occur during the strategy's start-up and planning phases. The Zambia NCS emphasized implementation during the finalization of strategy policies and legislation, document through training programmes and local demonstration strategies. In Pakistan, the NCS planning phase saw the beginnings of a Sustainable Development Policy Institute and environment cells in a number of line agencies of the national and provincial governments. National environment umbrella legislation was drafted and broad involvement in the strategy planning process affected the receptiveness of governments to change, including the establishment of environmental protection agencies in each of the provinces, and the initiation of provincial conservation strategies.

Early implementation might be targeted to specific problems which are disclosed during the definition of issues. In Uganda, for example, concerns were expressed about pollution as a consequence of the proliferation of plastic bags. The NEAP secretariat immediately drafted regulations to control their use. Often, positive actions are already being taken by governments or communities on an ad hoc basis as a result of separate initiatives. Strategy secretariats can seek to identify these as 'good news' stories and reinforce them in other ways as elements in the overall framework for action. It is particularly important that a strategy build upon the best of what is already existing in a country. Selective support for innovative activities and the facilitation of exchange and links between them can be essential elements of strategy implementation during the planning phase. Other actions at this stage, such as demonstration programmes and capacity-building during policy development, are discussed later in this chapter, along with the role of the strategy secretariat in implementation.

Basic requirements for implementation

The most difficult time for most strategies is when plans must be turned into action. Many strategies have not made the transition. In fact, about 70 per cent of all sectoral and thematic strategies in Africa over the past ten years have not been implemented; others have been only partially implemented. Worldwide, even the most

successful national strategies have seen many important components of their action plans be unsupported or overtaken by events. For some, the strategy process appears to have stopped dead following the preparation of the main document. This was the case with the Peruvian and Costa Rican NCSs.

A strategy can still be influential, even if it does not reach full implementation. Peru's NCS process stalled when the government changed. However, the draft strategy document provided a basis for Peru's national report to UNCED, a review of the TFAP, and a new proposal for a national system of protected areas. It also led to four regional conservation strategies (also halted by the unstable political situation).

Costa Rica's National Conservation Strategy for Sustainable Development (ECODES) also stalled when the government changed. But the informal networks of professionals formed during the process continue, and the intellectual influence of the strategy document – which has an ambitious cross-sectoral approach based on systems analysis – has been strong. It brought to national attention the debate about the sustainability of development. It provided a framework for the TFAP and the innovative National Biodiversity Institute (INBio); and it led the National Park Service to start working on the concept of buffer zones, and hence to a local sustainable development strategy for the Llanuras de Tortuguero. ECODES also resulted in the establishment of a National

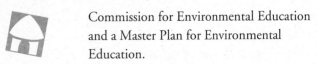

Commission for Environmental Education and a Master Plan for Environmental Education.

Experiences such as these would suggest that, to maximize the chances of full and systematic implementation, strategy teams should nurture:

- **Continuous high-level political backing:** It is here that the secretariat will need to be particularly strategic; targeting key leaders and groups of politicians for special attention. For example, at key points in implementation of the Nepal NCS, such as when the environmental assessment legislation was due to come before parliament, the NCS secretariat worked through journalist groups and other NGOs to conduct special awareness-raising seminars and discussion sessions with parliamentarians. Also, key decision-makers were taken to the sites of demonstration programmes, particularly those politicians whose constituents were benefiting directly from existing strategy activities. Ensuring the involvement of members of opposition parties is highly desirable, although not always easy when it is most needed.
- **Integration with recognized plans and procedure:** The strategy will carry more weight where is integrated with the national development plan and donor programming cycles than if it is treated as a one-off exercise.

- **Consistent and long-term sources of funds:** Ensuring that adequate funds are on tap when they are needed will take a good deal of secretariat time, resources and creative energy. Donors should be sensitive to the effort required and cater to this as a key element in secretariat work during early phases of the strategy. Sustainable financing is the goal, as discussed in Chapter 10.
- **The capacity for action:** Every proposed action brings with it a set of assumptions – often unwritten – about the capacities of the agencies or groups responsible for implementation; a frequent cause of failure in a strategy is that these bodies are not up to the job. Every substantive action called for in a strategy needs to be inextricably linked to supporting capacity-building programmes.
- **Coordinating mechanisms:** Effective coordination is particularly important in the early stages of implementation. A focal agency, often the strategy secretariat, will need to take on this role. As the strategy engages more participants, and as it progresses from cycle to cycle, coordinating functions should devolve to a range of agencies and levels of government. Some elements of implementation can be coordinated by the private sector or NGOs. Central monitoring will be important throughout.
- **Continuity:** The structures that provide the main energy force for strategy planning (for example) should remain in place during the transition to full

implementation while arrangements are made for their functions to be integrated permanently within the workings of government.

If there were an existing cabinet-level committee with responsibility for the strategy, this could continue as the overall coordinating and facilitating mechanism. If such a mechanism were not in place, then this is a desirable innovation, even if only as an interim or bridging mechanism during the crucial transition phase where many strategies have collapsed. In Pakistan, for example, a cabinet implementation committee was established immediately following approval of the NCS document.

Similarly, during the planning phase, the technical steering committee and secretariat would have acquired a deep familiarity with the issues, developed extensive networks and skills, and experienced team work: all invaluable resources during this difficult transition. In most strategies, these structures have been allowed to break down and their reservoir of experience and staff resources have dissipated before effective alternatives had been set in place. In Nepal, for example, the strategy secretariat ceased to exist for all practical purposes following the preparation of the NCS document. Some 18 months later it had to be recreated to build the implementation phase. It was another four years before an Environment Protection Council, chaired by the Prime Minister, was established, with the ultimate

responsibility for strategy coordination. A steady process of transferring secretariat responsibilities to the National Planning Commission and other agencies is still continuing.

This process of defining and transferring responsibilities, along with capacity development, takes time and needs to be viewed as an inherent part of implementation. The centres of energy for a strategy, which often have been painstakingly built up during planning, will be its most valued resources in implementation.

Implementation by national government

One of the key lessons of strategy experience is that it should be an ongoing process in which many of the components are repeated over a period of several years. Implementation will deepen and be expressed in many ways as different actors take up their roles, but a principal concern should be to fix all the elements of strategy planning within a country's existing development planning cycle. There may be a three- to ten-year planning cycle, but some countries rely principally on the annual budgetary cycle in defining development programmes.

Whatever the arrangement, a commitment will need to be made to reiterate the strategy planning process. This can be difficult if changes of government occur, which reinforces the need for a multipartisan approach

Box 20: Mediation, conflict resolution and arbitration: an Australian example

In Australia, the Commonwealth Environment Protection Agency (CEPA) was established as the central national body to implement the National Ecologically Sustainable Development Strategy process. It is required to work in close collaboration with the state and territory governments, industry, and the community to:

- determine clear national standards for and of indicators of sustainable development;
- develop well-defined processes for decision-making; and
- agree on effective consultative arrangements for better environmental management.

The CEPA works on establishing partnerships, decision-making methods and a policy framework that all Australian governments and sectors will respect. In 1989, the Resource Assessment Commission (RAC) was established to address the major issues which the strategy process had defined but on which consensus could not be reached. In carrying out its public inquiry functions, the RAC was guided by a set of policy principles (expressed in establishing legislation) for resolving competing claims and views over the use of resources. The principles are a useful model and, in summary, are:

- There should be an integrated approach, taking both conservation and development aspects into account at an early stage.
- Resource-use decisions should seek to optimize the net benefits to the community from the nation's resources, having regard to efficiency of resource use and environmental considerations, ecosystem integrity and sustainability, the sustainability of any development, and an equitable distribution of the return of resources.
- Government decisions, policies and management regimes may provide for additional uses that are compatible with the primary purpose values for the area; recognizing that, in some cases, both conservation and development interests can be accommodated concurrently or sequentially and, in other cases, choices must be made between alternative uses or combinations of uses.

In reaching consensus, or at least in coming to a position that the main parties can live with, the RAC interpreted these principles as demanding a thorough understanding of the range of beliefs and ethical frameworks underlying the different community values

box continues

relating to an issue. The RAC process aimed to ensure that even though a party may disagree with the final decision taken by a government, it accepts the reasonableness of the process which led to it. The major elements of the public inquiry process encompass research, clarifying the pertinent issues, meetings, public hearings, written submissions and the formulation of options and recommendations. Three important public inquiries undertaken by the RAC involved the sustainable use of forests, the management of Australian coastal zones and mining in a national park. A statutory authority such as the RAC is a valuable innovation in strategy implementation so that a body of expertise and a range of methodologies is built up to enable the consistent application of sustainable development principles to the resolution of major resource use issues.

Yet such an open process can threaten established development interests, and the RAC came under heavy attack from industry and opposition parties as a 'superfluous layer of green-tape bureaucracy' that drove away potential resource industry investors. The RAC was abolished four years after it began. The various sustainable development institutions, like all offspring of the strategy process, are likely to meet with strong resistance and, unless backed by committed and influential political constituency, can be short-lived.

Other desirable sustainable development structures include environment tribunals, which can mediate and, if necessary, arbitrate more specific conflict situations. These occur as strategy actions begin to define more sharply focused conflicts of interest over the use of specific sites or resources. The RAC was set up to examine national issues of conflict whereas other bodies, such as the Land and Environment Court within the Australian State of New South Wales, might conciliate on actions proposed within local strategies such as a zoning plan or the siting of an industry. Finally, administrative structures are needed to fulfill control and enforcement functions more akin to a conventional environment protection agency.

The precise form of these structures that seek to institutionalize strategies for sustainable development is not so important: in fact, one agency might fulfill any number of them. A greater concern is that there be a clear definition and understanding of their functions and relationships with other institutions, ie how they connect to the system.

to the process. Commitment to the strategy might best be expressed through a statutory obligation under an umbrella act relating to sustainable development. The reforms to government structure proposed in the strategy document may determine who will be responsible and how to manage the process.

Key sustainable development structures

It is essential that all agencies involved in implementing the strategy are clear about their relative responsibilities. The component actions are likely to be the responsibility of many bodies, both inside and outside government. The role and influence of the steering committee and secretariat or their equivalents (ie the central strategy agency) will vary. There will be:

- actions undertaken directly by the steering committee or secretariat – for example, certain demonstration and pilot projects, and communication and monitoring activities;
- actions influenced directly by the steering committee or secretariat, but undertaken by others – for example, major demonstration projects and activities of government sectoral agencies; and
- actions influenced only indirectly by the steering committee or secretariat – for example, corporate sector and individual initiatives in response to policies and incentives set by the strategy.

Choosing the central agency to drive implementation depends on how strategy planning was managed. In Nepal, the National Planning Commission provides the secretariat for the strategy and its overseeing body, the Environmental Protection Council (EPC). Similarly, in Zambia, the inter-sectoral EPC, which falls under the Minister of Environment, manages both the NCS and NEAP processes. A central strategy agency will need to have four main characteristics. It should:

1. be close to the action (ie closely related to the most powerful agencies or individuals in government, but also have links with grassroots institutions);
2. include a mechanism for high-level, credible, inter-sectoral links;
3. have a broad and flexible mandate which allows it to act as a catalyst, facilitator, demonstrator, and review body; and
4. be independent to help set in place transparent, consistent, impartial, participatory, and authoritative processes of mediation and conflict resolution in major resource issues.

Different levels of sustainable development structures and agencies established in Australia are described in Box 20.

A wide range of other structural reforms can complement and reinforce the functions of the central strategy agency. In the United States, two new executive offices have been established to coordinate the preparation of sustainable development policy. The Office for Environmental Policy focuses on domestic issues, while the Global Environmental Affairs Office, situated within the National Security Council, deals with international issues. Both report direct to the President and have a mandate to produce action plans that set out policies and approaches to implementation. They are required to seek broad public participation and inter-agency collaboration. Also, the US Environmental Protection Agency (EPA) has established a strategic planning group that examines critical development trends, and, on the basis of various future projections, identifies emerging environmental problems and their possible solutions.

In Pakistan, the Sustainable Development Policy Institute was established following the recommendation of the NCS. It has a monitoring and evaluation role in addition to identifying the main sustainable development issues and defining frameworks for public action.

Sustainable development law

Sustainable development structures, and the laws which underpin them, need to reflect the flowering of a comprehensive consultation and capacity-building process that begins during strategy planning and continues as part of implementation. This is particularly true for those laws that set in place the main institutional and decision-making framework for integrating the strategy process throughout government and the community. Rarely should laws be the point of departure in a strategy; rather, important signposts erected along the way so that the journey becomes a familiar and well-charted one for the communities concerned. It is particularly important that the technical officers and lawyers responsible for implementing the laws have had a central role in preparing them.

'If sustainable development is to mean anything at all, it will have to involve a partnership with the future, not just a partnership for profit.'

Chris Rose, Greenfreeze Project, UK

Law reforms will be needed at different levels of government and across sectors but the minimum content for a national system of sustainable development law should provide for:

Sustainable development principles and definitions, including a coherent philosophical framework that sets out the basic principles of sustainable development and the practical ways in which they will be applied (Box 21).

Recognition of the NSDS, including:

- legal commitment to the NSDS process;
- a commitment to revise and update the strategy policy framework (ie to repeat the strategy planning phase) regularly, for

Box 21: Principles for sustainable development law

A range of principles or approaches to sustainable development are now being expressed more frequently in international agreements and domestic legislation. Although they all encapsulate ideas that have been common in political philosophies for a long time, most have only recently been expressed as basic tenets of environmental policy.

Even the polluter pays principle, which goes back some 20 years, is only beginning to work through the decision-making system to have practical effect. The process has yet to begin in most developing countries. All these approaches are expressed in some form or other within the Rio Declaration and Agenda 21. The principles need to be cast in a way which reflects the cultural, political and economic nature of a country and the different communities within it. They work best when applied together, especially when special circumstances would mean that the rigorous application of one principle alone might be impracticable or inequitable.

The **public trust doctrine** has its origins in Roman Law. It has been extended in recent years, placing a duty on the state to hold environmental resources in trust for the benefit of the public. At its widest, it could be used by the courts as a tool to protect the environment from many kinds of degradation. In some countries, the doctrine has formed the basis of environmental policy legislation, allowing private rights of action by citizens for violations by the state (directly or indirectly) of the public trust.

The **precautionary principle** as defined in the Rio declaration holds that where there are threats of serious or irreversible damage, lack of full scientific certainty shall not be used as a reason for postponing cost-effective measures to prevent environmental degradation (or expressed more liberally, when in doubt about the impact of development, manage according to the worst-case scenario of its effect on the environment). Politically, this principle is difficult to apply and is, in fact, ignored in most countries. Erring on the side of caution is not an attractive option when considered against immediate projected economic benefits which can be spelt out in conventional development terms.

The **principle of inter-generational equity** is at the heart of the definition of sustainable development and requires that the needs of the present are met without compromising the ability of future generations to meet their own needs. It depends on the effective application of the other principles for sustainable development combined.

box continues

The **principle of intra-generational equity** requires that people within the present generation have the right to benefit equally from the exploitation of resources, and that they have an equal right to a clean and healthy environment. This principle applies to the relationship between groups of people within and between countries. This principle is being applied more and more in international negotiations. But within nations, it is particularly susceptible to cultural and socio-economic forces.

The **subsidiarity principle** is resurfacing worldwide after many decades of centralized planning and decision-making. In essence, it is the principle that decisions should be made by the communities affected or, on their behalf, by the authorities closest to them. Decisions should rest at the national rather than international level and local rather than national level. This has been the basic principle governing the devolution of planning systems worldwide and is intended to encourage local ownership over resources and responsibility for environmental problems and their solutions. These growing pressures for devolution in government need to be balanced by a recognition that local areas are part of larger systems and cannot function in isolation. Often, environmental problems may come from forces outside of local control, such as upstream pollution from a neighbouring country or community. In such cases, the other principles for sustainable development would override the subsidiarity principle.

The **polluter pays principle** (PPP) suggests that the polluter should bear the cost of preventing and controlling pollution. The intent is to force polluters to internalize all the environmental costs of their activities so that these are fully reflected in the costs of the goods and services they provide. Problems will be inevitable if an industry or plant would go out of business if this principle were enforced rigorously. A community might decide, for example, that the employment benefits of keeping a factory open outweigh the health and other environmental costs of pollution. Environmental agencies in developed countries have usually taken a flexible approach, with the continuation of government subsidies in special cases and the negotiation of individual programmes to allow certain polluters to meet new environmental standards gradually.

The **user pays principle** (UPP) applies the PPP more broadly so that the cost of a resource to a user includes all the environmental costs associated with its extraction, transformation and use (including the costs of alternative or future uses foregone). The PPP and UPP can be expressed in similar ways through market systems and government regulation.

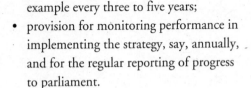

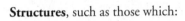

example every three to five years;

- provision for monitoring performance in implementing the strategy, say, annually, and for the regular reporting of progress to parliament.

Structures, such as those which:

- constitute the key sustainable development structures, defining their powers, functions, obligations, establishment and relationships with other institutions, ensuring that they are centrally placed and have influence in economic and development decision-making in government; and
- build strong links for communication and decision-making among sectors.

Environmental rights, involving a system of legal rights for people to take action to protect the environment, to require the government to act, to have access to information, to participate in policy-making and to question decisions.

Decision-making methods and processes, including:

- the requirement that all proposed new developments and new policies should be subject to environmental assessment;
- the use of economic incentives and disincentives, based on appropriate taxes, charges and other instruments;
- the requirement that industries, government departments and agencies be sub–

ject to periodic environmental audit; and
- effective monitoring, development control and enforcement and compliance mechanisms.
- accountability of government agencies and the private sector for their actions; and
- open and participatory methods for mediation, conciliation, conflict resolution and settlement of disputes for both broad fields of national policy and on more specific issues where consensus is lacking.

Promoting partnership, including systems that encourage partnerships for sustainable development between levels of government and with the private sector and non-government organizations.

What is possible, or even desirable, in sustainable development law will vary from country to country according to the cultural and political context. The issue of environmental rights is particularly sensitive and difficult for some countries to embrace. The rule of thumb is to seek to maximize the legal expression of these basic elements of sustainable development.

Promoting action through regulation

The bulk of existing environmental regulation is aimed at specific sectors of the economy, and specifies production, technology or emission standards to reduce environmental degradation or resource depletion. Regulations can be effective and economically efficient in promoting sustainable development actions when standards:

- are based on objective criteria and scientific knowledge;
- specify a level of performance rather than a particular design or technology (ie leave it to industry to come up with the most cost-effective technology to meet the standard);
- are reassessed periodically to incorporate advances in scientific knowledge and changes in society's aspirations, and to monitor their effectiveness;
- are set after comparing the benefits of environmental policies with the costs of achieving them; and
- are based on analysis of the entire product life cycle (from production of the raw material to end use of the final product), to identify the points of intervention that will deliver the greatest result for the least cost.

Regulations have their disadvantages, however. They are seldom the most cost-effective way to reach a given standard of environmental quality and studies in the United States suggest that they can be up to six times as costly as the least-cost alternative. This is because regulations that do not meet the above criteria are often inflexible, requiring polluters to adopt standard solutions even if they were able to find better alternatives. Furthemore, regulations do not

provide incentives for further improvement beyond the required standard. In contrast, economic instruments produce a financial incentive even as wastes are reduced, hence stimulating continual improvement.

Promoting action through economic instruments

In contrast to regulation, by which government aims to set rules to control the behaviour of resource users, market approaches address strategy implementation in a different way. Economic instruments aim to sensitize both producers and consumers toward responsible use of environmental resources and avoidance of pollution and waste, by internalizing environmental and social costs. They include taxes, charges, subsidies, deposit/refund schemes and tradeable permits. These are geared towards 'getting the prices right' so that environmentally and socially beneficial goods and services are not at a market disadvantage with respect to polluting or wasteful competitors. Sometimes, therefore, they need to be accompanied by regulations or other controls to ensure this.

Economic instruments can enable industry and other resource users to meet environmental standards in a cost-effective way, encourage them to do better than the standards require, and add their resources to those of government to maintain ecosystems. They can:

Box 22: Examples of market-based approaches for environmental policy

Brazil: Discontinuing fiscal and credit incentives for ranching has saved around US$300 million annually, while easing (although not eliminating) pressures for deforestation.

China: Economic instruments include fees to discourage pollution, the reform of resource prices and the planned application of environmental taxes. Certain industrial pollutants are subject to emission fees, collected by local environmental protection offices. Revenues are placed in banks and used to finance loans to firms for pollution control investments, covering 20–25 per cent of the requirements for this purpose.

Colombia: The Ministry of Development will support environmental improvements in industry through a credit line from foreign banks and international lending agencies. A Fund for Industrial Modernization will provide credits for business to buy new equipment. From 5 to 10 per cent of the fund will be used for environmental projects. Companies that invest in cleaner technologies will benefit from reductions in capital gains tax of up to 20 per cent.

India: Measures include income tax exemptions from donations to environmental institutions; a 50 per cent depreciation allowance for devices that minimize pollution or conserve resources; soft loans and investment allowances for pollution control equipment; pollution fees; and a levy on water use. Fertilizer subsidies have been removed, with exemptions for small farmers.

Indonesia: Pesticide subsidies accounted for almost 80 per cent of the retail price in 1985, creating a big incentive to over-use them. This resulted in widespread soil and water pollution and a rise in pesticide-resistant strains of pests. After a severe loss of rice production, all but four of the chemicals were banned. Subsidies were eliminated entirely by late 1988. This greatly reduced pesticide use in favour of integrated pest management systems, and saved more than US$120 million a year.

- harness market forces to encourage producers and consumers to achieve environmental objectives;
- stimulate the development of environmentally-sound technologies and products;
- reduce costs of enforcement; and
- generate revenue.

The important task is to set the prices or taxes at the right level and to introduce change gradually so that it does not result in severe economic dislocation. Subsidies, in particular, should only be used in special cases where severe environmental problems and issues of equity come into play. A common effect of subsidies is to place a significant economic burden on a country by supporting technological backwardness and inefficiency. Also, they often result in large-scale environmental damage by discouraging full internalization of costs. Economic subsidies with negative environmental effects should be removed.

Box 22 provides some examples of how economic instruments have been used to encourage implementation of environmental policies.

Interest in economic instruments to promote sustainable development actions has grown with the increasing concern about the efficiency of over-regulation. Yet there are circumstances in which economic instruments may not work or would need to be applied carefully in combination with other approaches, especially in lower-income economies:

When people are too poor to pay: Economic instruments that rely on governments charging fees or collecting taxes from polluters are unlikely to work in the majority of rural areas in lower-income countries, where poor people live in subsistence conditions and simply cannot pay. In these areas, positive subsidies or incentives should be considered.

When markets are undeveloped: In many poor countries, a combination of undeveloped markets, uncertainty about supply and demand, and macroeconomic instability undermines the effectiveness of market-based instruments.

Choosing the right policy tools to promote action

The OECD has adopted five criteria to judge whether economic instruments or regulations would best tackle a given environmental problem:

1. environmental effectiveness;
2. economic efficiency;
3. equity (for example, distributional effects in society of the instrument);
4. administrative feasibility and cost; and
5. acceptability (to groups who will be affected by the policy).

In most cases, tools from the three different approaches – regulation, cooperative processes, and economic instruments – will need to be applied together in combinations best suited to the situation. For example, regulations and voluntary agreements could set basic standards and targets while economic instruments could provide the stimulus to meet and exceed them by whichever means each business finds most efficient. Whatever the approach, there should be a policy transition, giving industry a stable and predictable climate in which to shift from unsustainable to sustainable practices.

Integration

Of central importance to strategy implementation are integrating mechanisms that build bridges between key agencies and groups participating in a strategy and that lead to partnerships and greater collaboration. They are needed to form working links between national government agencies, between levels of government, and between government, the private sector and the public. They are important because:

- positions and decisions are likely to be respected more broadly and be able to be implemented;
- priority issues identified in a strategy are usually cross-cutting, affecting many sectors;
- implementation is the responsibility of many agencies and often can only be undertaken jointly;
- agencies that have the central responsibility for coordinating an NSDS, such as environment ministries, often are weak and need to rely on collaboration and others' self-interest; and
- monitoring of progress in strategy implementation and enforcement, where powers have been introduced, requires partnerships and collaboration.

Integrating mechanisms can include structures like committees or working groups, various forms of agreements on the way things are to be done, and innovative decision-making methods that are inherently cross-cutting, such as environmental assessment.

Integrating structures

These can take many forms. The more important are underpinned by legislation but most operate on a more informal basis. In Canada's Yukon Territory, for example, the government has established a statutory Council on the Economy and the Environment, with members representing aboriginal people, labour unions, business, women, NGOs and a municipal government, bearing in mind the need for a balance of regions and interests in the territory. The council has a broad range of functions, including monitoring implementation of the Yukon Conservation Strategy. It is an advisory body to the territorial cabinet but can report directly to the territory's legislative assembly on certain matters.

The Nepal Environment Protection Council is similarly constituted and also oversees NCS implementation, reporting directly to the Prime Minister. In the UK, an independent group of experts from government and the private sector has been established to advise the Prime Minister on areas where policies and practices conflict with the environment objectives within the government's NSDS.

As implementation deepens, national and local strategies will need to be linked effectively through integrating structures. In

Panama, the Ministry of Planning and Economic Policy is represented on the coordination team of a local strategy (Bocas del Toro). This ensures that national planning takes account of the strategy's proposals and translates them into national budget allocations. The strategy for Petén, Guatemala, was developed by the Secretary for Economic Planning and adopted as the government's official plan. A regional forum of governmental and non-governmental organizations meets once a month to consider common problems and coordinate activities.

Existing consultative mechanisms – such as inter-agency committees, inter-governmental councils (such as the Environment and Conservation Council in Australia) and the many forms that bring together governments with other groups – should be reviewed for their potential to contribute to strategy implementation. Some might need strengthening if they lack sufficient credibility to contribute effectively. A number of innovative approaches have become the main creative driving force for planning and implementation. Structures which have co-evolved as variations on the same theme include:

Round tables: A round table is a group of senior representatives of government, business, citizens' groups and other key sectors of society. It provides a forum for collaborative analysis and treatment of major issues, educating government and NGO leaders in each other's perspectives, approaches and concerns. The group should be fairly small – ideally around 25 – although that may make it difficult to cover all the key sectors. The bigger the group, the more difficult it is to develop the right atmosphere for progress. In some cases, for example British Columbia's Strategy for Sustainability, the round table is also the steering committee of the strategy. In other cases, round tables are vehicles for discussing, developing and helping to implement the strategy, but overall direction of the strategy is the responsibility of a separate steering committee.

Core groups: A core group is an inter-sectoral network of government officials from most, if not all, ministries and departments. It provides a forum for bringing in sectors to deal with shared problems. The group may be large: Nepal's Environmental Core Group involves more than 70 people, its members coming together in differing combinations depending on the policy being addressed at the time; for example, environmental assessment procedures or national heritage conservation. A core group is a working network, intended to internalize the strategy (or aspects of the strategy) within government.

Action networks: These are networks of national government agencies, local governments, and non-governmental actors that come together to solve multi-sectoral problems, often in a particular part of the country, such as a river basin or a coastal zone. For example, an action network was formed to address problems of water pollution in the Densu River Basin in Ghana. As the problems change, the composition of the network changes. Because action networks are designed to address multi-sectoral issues, they are an important means of implementing an NSDS.

Round tables, core groups and action networks all seek to provide structures and processes for problem-solving and consensus-building beyond the conventional forms of government characterized by hierarchical, inflexible and closed decision-making. Most mediation and conflict resolution can continue within such informal and task-oriented networks and groupings. They allow participants from different organizations – who might not normally interact – to contribute as equal partners, to exchange experience, learn by doing and, through mutual support, build their own confidence and commitment to agreed actions. It is in governments' interest to facilitate, resource and acquire the skills to manage these new forms of partnership.

Integrating agreements

Agreements can be reached through conventional forms of negotiation or innovative networking. Usually the goal is to agree on collaborative ways of working that meet sustainable development objectives, often through self-management. When national

environment assessment legislation was introduced to Australia, Memoranda of Understanding were negotiated with all key sectoral agencies, detailing how each would take responsibility for applying the legislation to its own activities. Also, an Inter-Governmental Agreement on the Environment (IGAE) was adopted in 1992 to provide mechanisms for:

- a reduction in the number of disputes among the commonwealth and the states and territories on environmental issues;
- a cooperative national approach to the environment;
- a better definition of the roles of the respective governments;
- greater certainty of government and business decision-making; and
- better environmental protection.

The agreement embraces many of the principles of the National Ecologically Sustainable Development Strategy, and defines the roles and responsibilities of the different levels of government. Intra-generational equity is of particular concern to the Australian federation; the agreement sets in place a consultative structure for establishing national environment protection standards, guidelines, goals and associated protocols. The object is to ensure:

- that people enjoy the benefit of equal protection from air, water and soil pollution and from noise, wherever they live; and

- that decisions by business are not distorted and markets are not fragmented by variations among jurisdictions in relation to major environmental protection measures.

The implementation of national strategies can be greatly assisted by these kinds of governmental agreements. In fact, in many countries implementation is not possible without them. Voluntary agreements with the private sector are discussed later in this chapter.

Integrating mechanisms

In strategy implementation, the various forms of environmental assessment and planning are the most valuable methods of drawing together sectors and disciplines, and conservation and development issues. Some countries have developed national systems of environmental assessment and resource-use planning as part of the sustainable development management framework. By working cooperatively to develop these various decision-making methods, participants, such as sectoral experts, can gain a better appreciation of the environmental responsibilities of their own agencies vis-a-vis other sectors. Such cooperative efforts help people better understand the role of the central planning and environment organizations and improve working relationships between them.

Implementation by the strategy secretariat

The strategy secretariat, whatever form it takes, has a special role in implementation. Its principal concern needs to be setting in place the key ingredients of an institutional and decision-making framework for sustainable development at the national level. It should focus on the inter-sectoral aspects of the strategy which are not covered by, but affect all other, government agencies. In Nepal, the NCS secretariat implementation programme includes:

- building key environment institutions;
- setting in place a basic framework of sustainable development law;
- developing national systems of environmental assessment and pollution control;
- environmental education and public awareness;
- heritage conservation; and
- developing a national system and methods of environmental planning.

In pursuing these goals, the secretariat is using the environment core group approach and other integrating mechanisms to forge partnerships with the private sector and NGOs. This process was complemented and reinforced by selected demonstration and pilot programmes.

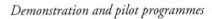

Demonstration and pilot programmes

The strategy secretariat may, at least in the first cycle of implementation, need to mount one or more pilot programmes to test and demonstrate the practical application of policies, and to build capacity and commitment within relevant sectors. These pilot programmes should generally aim only at inter-sectoral activities or those which fall outside existing sectoral mandates.

Demonstration and pilot programmes can be introduced at any point in the strategy cycle as model sustainable development activities. They can be particularly valuable when some of the proposed approaches (ie integration, coordination and participation) are unfamiliar or even threatening. In addition, they can enable the feasibility and effectiveness of various cross-sectoral approaches to be tested in local situations.

In certain countries, such as Zambia, Botswana and Nepal, the policy and institutional changes required by the strategy have not been made until several demonstration programmes have been underway for some time, and have shown the need and direction for change. Even where policy and institutional changes are made soon after preparation of the policy framework, demonstration programmes can provide ways to introduce new approaches. Without this initial focus activity, it is often difficult for several sectoral agencies to coordinate activities and define and achieve joint aims.

Demonstration projects can have a multiplier effect, helping people understand – far more than any document can – what the strategy is all about, and generating support for it. To fulfill this potential, a demonstration project should:

- have a high chance of success;
- show what it is intended to demonstrate (this is obvious but needs to be stated);
- be monitored closely;
- have quick results; and
- select its location and participants carefully to ensure both the success of the project and wide and rapid transference of the experience.

Often, pilot projects will build on an existing activity. In Zambia, two significant regions were selected as NCS pilot districts. These were areas where a number of sectors and interest groups shared problems: an urban area, the project for which was based on a successful NGO programme; and an agriculturally marginal rural area, for which a new project was specially developed.

Implementation through other strategies

A national strategy provides an umbrella of policies and a range of well-targeted actions; the most important concerning new instruments, methods and capacities for making better decisions. These policies and actions may reach across government and down to local levels, but will be given expression through more detailed planning and implementation.

Box 6 in Chapter 4 provides examples of the different strategy types. For example, depending upon the priorities of national government; thematic strategies, covering biodiversity, environmental education, climate change or population might be needed. These would cut across all government sectors and generate more comprehensive actions relating to the theme. Similarly, sectoral strategies will be needed to pick up on the momentum of policies and demonstration programmes of the national strategy. These will follow their own cycles and feed back to the broader national process.

In countries with a federal system, state or provincial governments may feel that the national strategy cannot be translated directly to local levels. They may feel that a greater sense of ownership and focus would come through a state or provincial strategy, once again building on and integrating with the national process. This is what is happening in Pakistan, although the way the links between the national and provincial conservation strategies will evolve is yet to be determined. In most countries, this crucial meshing of strategy cycles will come only through trial and error and exchange of experience with other countries.

Core groups or action networks have an important role to play, complemented by the kind of integrating structures, agreements and methods previously described. In countries with very large populations, such as India, or even the United States, the state or provincial level will need to be given special emphasis in providing the strategy umbrella for fostering local initiatives. In countries with a regional structure, such as New Zealand and Nepal, actions within the national strategy process will need to stress the subsidiarity principle. In Nepal, the National Environmental Planning Guidelines prepared by the NCS environment core group drew from the experience of eight local conservation strategies undertaken as pilot exercises. They reinforced the government's policies on devolution and promotion of district- and local-level strategies.

A central component of New Zealand's strategy for sustainable development is the Resource Management Act, introduced to devolve major sustainable management functions to regional councils. The councils are required to initiate their own strategy processes. A number of the state governments in Australia have introduced similar systems, placing the main responsibilities for policy definition and implementation with local government.

In a number of developed countries, the strategy processes tend to merge with the conventional land-use planning systems as they come closer to local communities. In many less developed countries, planning for land-use tends to proceed in isolation from planning for social services. Strategy processes can bring them back together.

In Australia's Victoria State, more than 20 local governments have mounted local conservation strategies based on the National Ecologically Sustainable Development strategy model and following guidelines prepared by the state government. Local sustainable development strategies are the subject of a separate handbook in the IUCN series.

Implementation by the non-governmental community

Whatever the strategy level, much of the implementation should be non-governmental; by business and industry, schools and universities, research institutions, environmental organizations, human development organizations, community groups, and so on. The wealth-creating sectors of society are almost entirely outside government; so it is essential that business and industry be centrally involved in implementing the national strategy. Much societal organization and mobilization occurs via the host of non-market, non-governmental organizations, so they must implement the strategy too.

Input from the earliest stage

Businesses and NGOs are unlikely to become involved in implementation unless

they have a sense of ownership of the strategy. It is vital that they participate in the choice of objectives and issues, assembly and analysis of information, policy formulation, and decisions on the strategy. Some strategies are, by design, basically governmental: they are meant to be implemented primarily by the national government. The Malaysian NCS is an example. Others are intended to be implemented more widely. The action plan of the Pakistan NCS, for example, includes many actions by business and industry. However, the corporate sector was involved only marginally in formulating and deciding the Pakistan NCS and so was not ready to implement the strategy when it was adopted by government. An industry round table has now been established to work through the main fields and methods for action.

The Pakistan experience highlights the strength of the target group approach adopted by the Netherlands' National Environmental Policy Plan (NEPP), in which industry, farmers and other non-governmental sectors are included as partners with government. The non-governmental partners share in diagnosis and setting targets, and undertake much of the implementation through voluntary agreements.

Cooperation rather than compulsion

The trend in the relationship between government and industry, in particular, is to seek cooperation rather than forcing implementation of strategy policies through complex regulatory frameworks. Experience has taught that, where industry has assisted in identifying the key environmental problems, it is more likely to recognize its shared responsibility for tackling them. The main components of the cooperative approach are:

- establishing an action network or core group;
- reaching an agreement defining the cooperative actions; and
- reinforcing the agreement through incentives for action, and agreed and credible penalties for lack of action.

In the United States, this approach is being seen as a substitute for the lengthy and expensive regulatory approach, which often involves extensive litigation. In the energy sector, for example, the use of 'collaboratives' followed by voluntary 'settlements' is now facilitating the implementation of sustainable development strategies in industry. It is also helping overcome the antagonism resulting from what industry had labelled the BANANA syndrome: Build Absolutely Nothing Anywhere Near Anything. The US Federal Energy Regulatory Commission defines 'collaboratives' as a group of individuals from government, NGOs and the private sector who pool resources to constructively solve problems without recourse to litigation. Independent facilitators have often been used to help in

discussions and, in particular, to reach the negotiated settlements.

In upper-income countries, voluntary agreements are increasingly becoming part of environmental policy because they can provide more flexible and cost-effective ways for government and industry to meet environmental goals. Their use in lower-income countries is limited but growing. Pioneered through the concept of self-regulation and industry codes of practice, more companies are committing themselves to improving their environmental performance. In many cases, the pressure to do so comes from employees, consumers, investors and local communities. Companies find it is in their longer-term self-interest to take action. Advantages of the voluntary approach are:

- voluntary commitments do not, of course, have to be vague or go unrecognized – precise industry standards for environmental performance and quality control have been established (such as British Standard 7750 and the ISO 14000 Series), which help with public/market recognition of voluntary efforts;
- industry is encouraged to define least-cost actions for meeting the agreed standards;
- the costs to government of setting in place regulatory systems are reduced;
- the chances of implementation are increased; and
- a more constructive relationship between

industry, government and NGOs is established, reducing delays to development.

In the UK and Japan, industries are encouraged to introduce Environmental Management Systems on their own initiative. Such systems can enhance their public image and the marketability of their products and reduce the likelihood of government taking punitive actions.

Such agreements and voluntary systems are, however, successful only if they are backed up with a government intention to regulate if industry performance does not meet the environmental goals within an agreed time scale. Voluntary initiatives are particularly difficult in marginal industries or in countries where a depressed economic situation discourages immediate action to improve environmental performance. In such cases, the cooperative approach would need to be accompanied by strong legislation and/or well-targeted incentive measures.

Building capacity

Building capacity for sustainable development is a central task of national strategies. It requires developing the necessary individual and group perspectives, skills and organization. Capacities are needed through all the main components of a strategy: for assessment, including diagnosis (at the start of a strategy), and monitoring and evaluation (during the entire strategy cycle); for

designing the actions (planning); and for taking the actions (implementation).

Capacity-building needs to respect the same principles which govern the entire strategy process and which have been enunciated throughout this handbook. They relate to ways of changing or strengthening societal values, knowledge, technologies and institutions. Capacity-building applies equally to strengthening and improving governmental and non-governmental organizations of all kinds, from national to local levels. The increased capacities should lead to communities that are more self-reliant and equitable, and more open, participatory and integrated in their decision-making.

Three main types of capacity are needed at the national level:

1. Mechanisms for cross-sectoral communication, policy development and decision-making. These include participatory approaches to conflict resolution and consensus-building, improved networking, and structures and tools to facilitate coordination and collaboration.
2. Methods for integrating different environmental, social, and economic perspectives and objectives. These include approaches to planning, assessment, decision-making and information systems.
3. Ways of bringing government agencies and the non-governmental community to understand and fulfill their own environ-

mental and social responsibilities. They include furthering awareness and environmental education, research, learning-by-doing approaches, the design and handling of instruments for environmental management, monitoring and forecasting, and the application of new environmental technologies.

Early action builds capacity

An effective way of building capacities is to take action – from the earliest stages of a strategy – on those aspects to which participants are already committed. Experience in Nepal has shown that if actions are taken in policy areas that do not threaten the territorial imperative of key government sectors, then a strategy secretariat can do much to increase technical capacities and political commitment. In this case, key staff from many government sectors were involved in the development of a national system of environmental assessment. This resulted in broader thinking on environmental policy generally and a better understanding of how it is applied. It also led to the establishment of environment units within many ministries and an Environment Protection Council.

Implementing an EA programme such as Nepal's, at the same time as developing the strategy's policy framework, brings a number of important benefits to the strategy process. It:

- exposes sectoral experts to environmental or developmental problems in ways that are of immediate relevance to their work;
- increases their understanding and skills in inter-disciplinary fields, such as environmental management methods;
- forges working links among sectors and with the environment agencies on development issues;
- makes their input to the strategy policy framework more informed;
- engenders commitment to policy implementation;
- increases the chance that momentum in the strategy process will be maintained during the transition from policy formulation to action and will survive changes in government;
- creates a network of sectoral expertise, through which implementation can proceed within existing institutional arrangements; and
- achieves (it is hoped) better, more sustainable decisions as a direct result of EA.

An emphasis on capacity-building as a way of developing important areas of environment policy begins to shrink the considerable gap that often exists between policies, as expressed in various development plans and in practice. Such an emphasis forces technical staff to confront, for example, the incompatibility among policies that require decentralized mechanisms, devolved authority and cross-sectoral collaboration and the management style of their own institutions, which is most

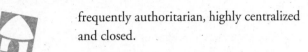

frequently authoritarian, highly centralized and closed.

Building capacity in the non-governmental and private sectors

---

'Environmental debate and environmental education can go on for ages, but while poverty-ridden communities do not have benefits, we are talking to an unconverted group.'

Taparendava Mavaneke, CAMPFIRE Project, Zimbabwe

Capacity-building and implementation should embrace the corporate sector, NGOs and communities as well as government. Historically, the government has been seen as the primary agent to induce and maintain the social and economic changes required for the overall task of nation-building. By and large, such work has concentrated on increasing the skills, knowledge and professional capacities of public servants. Increasingly, evaluations have shown that the performance of government development projects and programmes is critically dependent on the functioning of both state institutions and NGOs. More recent strategies realize this: for example, the Papua New Guinea Forestry and Conservation Action Plan gives equal emphasis to the building of non-governmental and government capacity. It recognizes that NGOs are crucial in organizing and 'brokering'

government services to the traditional land-owners, who own 97 per cent of the land.

A particularly valuable role for strategy implementation is demonstrating and testing development options that emphasize sustainable use of resources by communities or small private enterprise. The NCS implementation programme in Nepal, for example, includes a fund to help community cooperatives and NGOs identify sustainable uses of their resources as an alternative to existing, more damaging developments.

Technical backing is provided in the management, accounting and monitoring of these small enterprises and in the initial assessment of alternatives to define benign but profitable enterprises. Successful marketing of new products, such as hand-made papers, traditional cloth, soaps or artwork, often holds the key to sustainabilty. It requires special measures to promote economic partnerships; often well beyond the boundaries of the community concerned. The principles governing sustainable use in these situations – and the processes which can ensure they are upheld – need to be defined in close collaboration with the communities or groups that must apply them.

Government should create an enabling environment for sustainable development in all sections of society, not just the state.

NGOs can be effective carriers of sustainable development throughout the country; catalyzing participation, organizing and mobilizing groups, obtaining grassroots perspectives, raising awareness, and providing long-term ideas, analysis and advocacy. Building non-governmental capacities for sustainable development is as important as building governmental capacities. To work effectively with government, NGOs need simple funding and administrative mechanisms that do not compromise their independence.

Conclusion

Achieving an early focus in implementing a national strategy will depend upon the extent to which basic needs are being met. Where the private sector and NGOs are barely developed and government is highly centralized, a strategy should be very selective in what it attempts to achieve at the different levels of society. It might be most important to show results in development terms within selected communities so that the strategy constituency continues to grow. In countries that enjoy a higher level of human well-being, strategies can promote more ambitious actions that require longer-term perspectives of environmental maintenance. Whatever the level of economic development or sophistication of decision-making institutions, experience with strategy implementation suggests three approaches to management, particularly within government.

First, it needs to be open and collaborative. In implemention, the most effective forms of decision-making are those which involve interest groups in sharing problem-solving; which go beyond sectoral boundaries; and which are flexible and organic. Forms of government are needed that build on the best in traditional approaches, that are transparent and form working unions with and between groups that normally function separately.

Second, management needs to be adaptive. Strategies for sustainable development are best viewed as processes for managing and adapting to change. Never before has the need for, and the pace of, change been so great. Forces influencing change include population growth, massive movements of people from hills to coastal and to urban areas; technological innovations that enhance people's ability to shape the environment; and, increasingly more significant, changes associated with environmental debts passed from one community or generation to another.

Even in the most self-sufficient, stable communities, background levels of change are inevitable. Strategies to cope with change are required. Communities satisfied with their level of development, or committed to conserving the essential elements of their environment and lifestyle, may wish for minimal change. Such communities, whether in Indonesia or Switzerland, would seek to maintain most elements of their natural and cultural heritage while making selective changes to certain qualities of life. The emphasis is not on permanent strategies for the years or decades to come. Rather, adaptive strategies are required in which all goals and actions are continually re-evaluated.

Third, management needs to be conciliatory. As national strategies begin to take effect, conflict between development options and interests will become better defined. Such conflict is frequently disruptive, but need not be. It can be managed so as to contribute to social integration and innovation. It can facilitate communication and define relationships and group structures in order to clarify for people their position relative to others. At this produc-

tive level, conflict can be used to initiate direct interaction among affected groups, through specific and accepted procedures that lead to the negotiation of settlements. Increasingly, institutions within and outside government will be needed to facilitate these processes of conciliation and mediation, so that mutually acceptable and respected settlements assist sustainable development.

Crucial to these voluntary processes is the information that flows from a constant assessment of the changes taking place in society and its environment. Gathering information, analyzing it and making prescriptions for settlement of conflicts holds the key to keeping strategies on track, and is the subject of the next chapter.

Chapter 9

Keeping Strategies on Track

Assessment combines monitoring, evaluating and reporting on the strategy. Assessment is primarily forward-looking; its purpose is to improve the strategy process, help it meet objectives and adapt it to changing needs.

Assessment should be an integral part of the strategy from the start and cover all aspects: objectives, participation, communication, role in the decision-making system, planning, implementation and results.

This chapter outlines an approach to assessing progress toward sustainable well-being. It is intended to be used by the people who advise, or in some way influence decision-makers involved in strategies.

As the national strategy process begins to take hold, it will need to be expressed in linked strategies at many levels: the household, farm, municipality, business, province or nation – anywhere that 'stakeholder' groups, or combinations of these, try to improve or maintain the well-being of people and ecosystems. The approach is meant to apply to assessment of all such strategies. Hence its essentials are simple and few. Details will vary from strategy to strategy, depending on the people and ecosystems involved. To make the main points clear, the chapter includes only a basic discussion.

The approach to assessing sustainability is described in five sections:

1. *the purpose of assessment;*
2. *assessing the progress of society/ecosystem interactions;*
3. *assessing the progress of a particular strategy;*
4. *participation in assessment; and*
5. *making assessments useful.*

The purpose of assessment

Assessments are essential for the success of any strategy, regardless of its scale or scope, or the education and income of its participants. Assessment is the process of judging progress toward the goal of sustainable development or well-being; asking and answering key questions about:

- human and ecosystem well-being, and their interactions and trends, so that the various strategy constituencies may progressively define, agree on and revise objectives and a strategy to achieve them; and
- the progress of the strategy itself, so that participants may improve its design and operation.

Assessment is best understood as a composite of various functions that are already well-known to strategy practitioners. In broad terms, these include the following processes and questions:

- **Monitoring.** What is happening?
- **Evaluation.** Is what was supposed to happen actually happening?
- **Analysis.** What should be happening now, and in the future?

The broader purpose of assessment is to evaluate and improve the progress society is making toward sustainable development or well-being. Its specific purpose is to enable people to:

- increase their understanding of human and ecosystem well-being and how to improve and maintain them;
- know what state they and their supporting ecosystems are in;
- determine where they and their supporting ecosystems are going;
- define where they want to be, and integrate/trade-off objectives;
- chart a course for getting there; and
- change that course in response to changes in conditions, information, values and priorities.

Assessment is an effort to determine which potentials exist and which could be improved and how (not simply what is wrong). Since sustainable development is a dynamic process, and sustainable well-being a dynamic condition, any strategy for sustainability must also be dynamic. Regular assessment enables the strategy to both respond to, and influence, changing conditions.

Who should do the assessment?

Two groups should undertake assessments: the stakeholders (people directly concerned) and independent outsiders. They do not have to do it together: 'internal' assessments by stakeholders are essential; 'external' assessments by others are desirable. The people directly concerned have most to gain from an assessment. They should be centrally involved; by participating in the assessment, they will know better what to do to achieve their objectives, and why. For a given set of decision-makers – at the level of the town, region or country – the emphasis placed on any particular topic, or the choice of specific measures, will vary depending on local conditions and priorities. Thus, it is essential that assessment of progress toward sustainability be driven by local participants.

At the same time, unbiased opinion and independent analysis can make a critical contribution to understanding. An external assessment can give stakeholders new insights, and avoid or overcome conflicts of interest involved in self-assessment.

When should assessments be done?

Assessment should be an integral part of decision-making. It should be a regular and integral activity rather than a sporadic and separate event and should, by and large, be done through normal operations, eg of management, to keep its potentially high costs within limits. Frequency of assessment will depend on how rapidly and significantly conditions are changing, and the magnitude of the risk to human or ecosystem well-being.

Assessment should be undertaken from the start, to create a baseline; and regularly thereafter as an integral part of any strategy. Assessment is implicit in the design and implementation of successful strategies. For example, an effective national strategy begins with the assessment of the strategy's

objectives and of the procedure for its design or formulation. Assessment continues throughout strategy formulation and implementation, covering both the relevance of the objectives and how they are being addressed: it also determines any revisions to the strategy.

The benefit of regular explicit assessment is that it encourages participants to rethink priorities, reset objectives, and rechart their course of action.

What should be assessed?

Assessment should provide and analyze two sets of information:

1. progress of society/ecosystem status and interactions toward sustainable well-being; and
2. progress of particular strategies toward their objectives and their contribution to the goal of sustainable well-being.

Assessing the progress of society/ecosystem status and interactions

The information that follows addresses both the broader social, economic and ecological context within which a strategy operates, and also some very specific criteria chosen to highlight the precise nature of people–ecosystem status and interactions. Four categories are suggested: ecosystems, people, interactions between people and ecosystems, and the synthesis of these. Each of the first three categories is portrayed as a hierarchy of information, ranging from specific measures at the bottom to complex systems at the top that build on and incorporate the lower levels (Figures 5, 6 and 7).

Ecosystems

The overall ecological goal is to maintain or improve ecosystem well-being. Assessment of progress toward this goal needs to consider the state of the ecosystem as a whole as well as selected resources, issues and criteria, such as air quality, water quality, soils, and plant diversity (Figure 5).

People

The goal is to improve or maintain human well-being. Assessment of progress toward this goal needs to consider the state of society as a whole as well as selected indicators, such as health, wealth, and happiness (Figure 6).

Figure 5: Ecosystem information levels

Ecosystem condition

The ecosystem is classified as one or a combination of the following:

Natural	**Modified**	**Cultivated**	**Built**
Slight human influence: the scale and rate of human impact are of the same order as the impact of other organisms.	Moderate to heavy human influence: not cultivated but human impact is greater than that of other species	Human-dominated: more than 50% cultivated	Human-centred: 50% covered by roads, buildings or other human structures

Climate and air	**Water**	**Land**	**Plants, animals and other biota**

Lower and more specific levels of information

For example: outdoor air; indoor air; groundwater; surface water; marine waters; soil; minerals; geology; primary productivity; biodiversity

Interactions between people and ecosystems

The goal is for human activities to increase or maintain benefits or values from ecosystems while reducing stresses on them. Assessment of progress toward this goal needs to consider: how and to what extent human activities contribute to the provision of basic needs and the quality of life; how these activities are valued; how they stress or help to restore the ecosystem; and progress in meeting the goal through legislation, incentives, and other measures (Figure 7).

Synthesis

The goal is sustainable well-being. Analysis of the first three categories is likely to show that some aspects of the ecosystem, society and their interactions are getting better, others worse, and others are about the same. The most important aspects and the main links between them need to be identified to arrive at an overall picture of the state of human and ecosystem well-being. Two forms of synthesis may be required: a macro-level set of indicators akin to, for example, the UN Human Development Index; and sample micro-level indicators at the sector, landscape, community or livelihood system level.

Assessing the progress of a particular strategy

A strategy is an evolutionary process, developing as it goes along and adapting to change. It is also cyclical, its main components – constituency-building, agenda-building, design, implementation and assessment – being repeated as it develops (Figure 8).

This means that a strategy need not and should not try to do everything at once. It

Figure 6: Society information levels

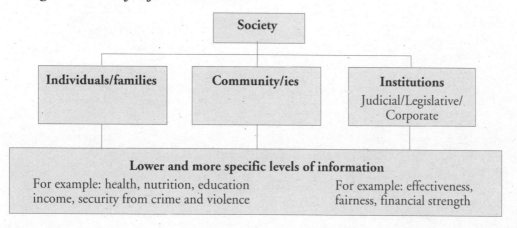

can grow in scope, ambition and participation as objectives are achieved (or changed) and as capacities to undertake the strategy are built.

Assessment of a strategy needs to cover four main aspects:

> *1. Participants in the strategy; objectives of the strategy; and their relationship*

Constituency-building and agenda-building should go together throughout the strategy. The participants decide the objectives, and the objectives determine the participants.

Assessment should ask: Who are the stakeholders? What are their interests? Are interests being dealt with equitably? Who are the 'winners' and the 'losers'? Are the interests of different groups compatible with the goal of sustainable development and well-being? If not, how can they be made compatible?

> *2. Communication among participants, and between participants and others*

Communication is the lifeblood of a strategy; the means by which participants exchange information with each other, reach

Figure 7: People-ecosytem information levels

Monitored activities			Non-monitored activities		
Goods	Services	Non-market	Household	Voluntary	Underground*
Combinations of monitored and non-monitored activities For example: energy use; water use; tourism and recreation					

Stress	**Benefit or value**
Physical Chemical Biological	Material Non-material

Lower and more specific levels of information	
For example: land use changes, erosion and sedimentation, noise, extraction, introduction of exotics (costed where relevant)	For example, value-added, employment, self-worth, pride, ritual, spiritual (costed where relevant)

Underground: Clandestine, black market, illegal and similar activities

agreement with each other on actions, change or strengthen values and impart knowledge, and inform others about the strategy. It is necessary to assess the modes, frequency and effectiveness of communication, both among participants, and between the participants and others.

3. What actions are planned, decided on and taken, and by whom; and what are the obstacles?

Actions are likely to be taken if priorities are clear, the number of top priority actions is practicable, the actors are identified, the required resources are specified, and the resources are allocated or their probable sources identified. Assessment needs to ask:

- who participates/participated, and how do/did they participate, in (a) assessment, (b) designing the actions, (c) deciding the actions, and (d) taking the actions?
- what actions were (a) assessed as high priority, (b) designed, (c) decided, and (d) taken?

- what were the reasons for any discrepancy among actions assessed as high priority, planned actions, actions to be taken, and actions that were taken: ie what actions did not have majority agreement, or were considered difficult to implement?
- what were the obstacles to making priority actions effective and how could they be overcome?

4. Effectiveness in terms of the strategy's objectives and the goal of sustainable well-being

This requires coordination between strategy monitoring and the society/ecosystem monitoring described above. Actions called for and taken as part of a strategy usually entail changing or strengthening one or more of:

- values (and habits);
- knowledge;
- technologies (and infrastructure);
- institutions (laws, incentive systems and organizations); and
- market conditions, eg price.

Figure 8: Strategy components

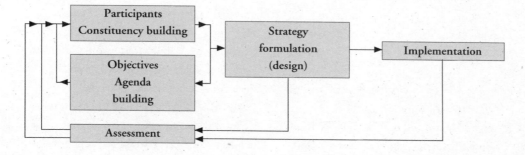

Any intended changes and improvements need to be identified clearly. Assessment will require an accurate description of the baseline situation (the people/ecosystem status assessment). To assess the impact of the actions on the strategy objectives, and to distinguish their impact from the effects of other factors, it is necessary to:

- clearly define the variables by which the strategy objectives are to be measured;
- monitor changes in these variables (through the people/ecosystem assessment);
- understand the relationship among the strategy objectives and values (and habits), knowledge, technologies (and infrastructure) and institutions – together with the relative importance of different factors (eg particular institutions); and
- determine the effect of the actions on values, knowledge, technologies and institutions.

Box 23 illustrates a range of questions used to monitor progress by a local strategies team in Pakistan.

Participation in assessment

The 'how' of assessment consists of two components:

1. how to use a participatory process to define the key questions; and
2. how to choose and use the right tools to help participants answer these questions.

People will often focus on the second component at the expense of the first, believing that the question of what is to be looked for it is already answered. Yet, repeatedly, attempts at assessment fail because those charged with the task do not ask themselves what questions need to be asked. They can establish this only by involving all the people who are affected by the issue. It is not possible to be prescriptive about the kinds of questions which strategy teams will need to ask.

Principles for participation

Assessments of progress toward sustainable well-being may be undertaken by corporations, communities, provinces, nations, or groups of nations. There will always be a role for scientific assessment – measurement of air, water, soil and biodiversity quality, etc. The real issue, however, is gaining an understanding of the evolving relationship between society and environment, and such assessments require broad-based participation. Regardless of who undertakes them, key rules or principles for guiding participatory assessments are:

Start with the story: If you want to learn what the problems are, don't ask what the problems are. Ask what the story is and the problems will become evident. Start with developing a consensus about the story (or stories, if a single consensus proves impossible) of the community, corporation, nation or area being addressed. Use this

Box 23: Assessment in a local strategy in Pakistan

Insight into national strategy progress may be gained through a sampling of local strategies. A major, long-term strategic project in three districts of Pakistan aims to arrest environmental degradation and improve natural resource-use through participation. This seven-year activity, which is in its early stages, is a collaborative venture involving the Governments of Punjab and North West Frontier Province, IUCN-Pakistan, IIED and the European Commission. It will proceed through community baseline assessment of local resources, needs and problems; ie assessment itself will be a focus for the social organization required for sustainable development. This will lead to community organizations forming at, for example, village, social group (women) and resource-user group level, and thence to participatory planning. Assessment of progress will be a judicious mix of scientific assessments; participatory monitoring of the economic, ecological, social and institutional systems surrounding the local strategy. Indicators are currently being explored. They should provide the following information on how the project is meeting its sustainability aims:

What should be assessed?

Economic sustainability:

- Is the economic productivity of degraded land improving, and are economic activities building on natural resource potentials?
- Are input/output ratios and subsidies for external inputs decreasing?
- Are production, processing and storage losses being minimized?
- Is the local economy diversifying?

Ecological sustainability:

- Is natural resource production combined with conservation (of soil, water, and wild/domesticated biological diversity), to ensure resilience?
- Are harvests constant or increasing, but not at the expense of conservation?
- Is the use of ecological processes optimized (eg biological nitrogen fixation, waste assimilation, and recycling of water and nutrients)?
- Is pollution minimized, both on-farm and off-farm?
- Are environmentally damaging practices being phased out?
- Are natural resource limits and potentials becoming better understood, and regularly monitored?

box continues

Social sustainability:

- Are natural resource use systems increasing people's control over their own lives and the range of choices open to them; and are they compatible with local values (eg taste and taboos) and systems of decision-making?
- Are the costs and benefits of natural resource rehabilitation and use equitably distributed so more people have access to resources for shelter, energy, materials and food, or so they have incomes to pay for these basics? And are special efforts made to redress imbalances, notably those disfavouring women?
- Is there a growing body of commonly-held knowledge on natural resource limits and opportunities, and is there increased local innovation in natural resource use?
- Is there a growth in local (para) professional capacity, capable of conducting natural resource research and planning?
- Is the farmer playing a leading role in rehabilitation and natural resource systems?
- Are people who used to rely on unsustainable activities for their livelihood being supported in their transition to sustainable activities?
- Is there a tendency toward full employment, with suitable off-farm employment to take the pressure off the land?

Institutional sustainability:

- Is local environmental rehabilitation taking place against a background of supportive, stable policy, ie, internal institutions (community rules and norms on resource allocation, multiple use, cost and benefit sharing, conflict resolution, and pursuing other collective natural resource values) and external institutions (government land tenure, revenue policy, social support systems, natural resource technical support systems, and infrastructure)?
- Are communities developing a diverse institutional support network in environmental rehabilitation — including government and the private sector — or are they over-reliant on one project?

Choice of indicators

One possible way to assess progress on these elements of sustainability is to focus on a few indicators, each of which covers the interaction of economic, ecological, social and institutional dimensions. These indicators will be fully developed during the community planning process, since they must be consistent with local strategy aims:

box continues

- **Changes in productivity:** Yields, resource conservation measures, costs.
- **Changes in resource quality:** Extent of resource-conserving practices; use of ecosystem functions; extent of resource-degrading practices; extent of local contribution to conservation technology development.
- **Changes in local resilience and vulnerability:** Agricultural and wild products managed and farmed, access to credit, impacts of drought on livelihood, human health).
- **Changes in self-dependence of groups and communities:** Extent of participation, local skills and capacities, effectiveness of local resource management/rehabilitation groups, dependence on external resources.
- **Replication of strategy successes at non-strategy sites:** Replication rates by neighbours, federation of groups to tackle broader-scale issues.
- **Changes in operations of support institutions:** New roles for professionals, enabling policies, increasing links with other agencies, local commitment to increasing capacity.

mechanism to involve people from all parts of the community, especially anyone with a sense of history.

Build a broader community of interests: The different groups of decision-makers involved in the issues being assessed may not feel that they share interests. Ways of bringing them together into a common interest group include:

- identifying a broader community – by looking for other people who share the same or similar problems, the community can become broader and more powerful and understand its own problems better;
- act, don't just talk – the sense of a community of interests and the under-standing of its members can best be developed through joint activities, and communities that are brought together purely through talk are less likely to hold together; and
- look for 'positives' in common, ie those changes that the majority agree have improved their well-being and that of the environment; success stories will be important for keeping the strategy on track. Equally, a minimum base of community consensus can also be established by identifying those things that all participants agree they are against.

Recognize value differences: Although the community of shared interests is broader than people think, unavoidable conflicts often exist between the interests, needs and values of individuals, the local community, other communities or the larger society. It wwis better to bring these out into the open rather than present an illusory consensus.

Understand communication: At all levels, from conference papers to posters and television, it is essential to understand the media and the audience. Without such understanding, communication will not work (see Box 13).

Tools for participation

Although each of the tools for assessment – from thermometers to questionnaires – has its place, a few key considerations apply to the selection of tools:

- **Learning by doing:** We may break into the cycle of design-action-assessment at any point. Prolonged diagnostic exercises involving extensive questionnaires and paper studies usually yield fewer insights than a handful of thoughtful projects in which implementation is seen as a technique for learning. Action-oriented research and participatory inquiry are useful means (see Box 9).
- **Maps:** Maps of all kinds, from satellite images to sketches drawn on the ground, are powerful tools to understand problems, monitor change and communicate proposals. Although people unused to maps can experience problems, in most cultures simple map creation and reading is a skill that can be acquired quite easily.

- **Meaningful indicators:** Informative indicators can be developed only when we are clear about the question we are asking. A few well-chosen indicators are likely to be more useful than volumes of comprehensive statistics. Indicators should emerge from discussion and, where possible, should be those that people are already using. In many rural communities, indigenous technical knowledge can often supply more precise and revealing indicators of evolving society/ecosystem relationships than externally-defined 'scientific' indicators.
- **Qualitative surveys:** Assessment systems often focus on the accumulation of quantitative data. Although such data can be important, generally it needs to be accompanied by studies that reveal the story behind the numbers. A few anecdotal stories revealing how environmental change is affecting individual families or communities will illuminate the data and can often be more informative than extensive surveys.
- **Open-ended questions:** However thoroughly the problem has been discussed and however carefully the indicators are selected, the most useful information may be that which we are not looking for; the unexpected insightful observation that suddenly puts the problem in a new light. Questions should be phrased in ways that encourage comment rather than simply yes/no responses. Assessments should be structured in ways that throw people together in combinations from which

new overlaps of knowledge and interest may emerge.

Making assessments useful

A useful assessment improves decision-making and facilitates action. It can do this, however, only if it provides information that helps decision-makers identify, agree on, and take such action.

Decision-makers, whether individuals, communities, corporations, or governments, have three needs in common with respect to assessment of sustainability:

1. **Relevance:** The assessment must focus on issues that are relevant to the concerns, needs and priorities of the decision-maker.
2. **Capacity to act:** The decision-maker must be able to do something about the information provided by the assessment. Land-user families cannot do anything with information on ozone depletion. Business leaders cannot improve the sustainability of their operations with information on the crime rate.
3. **Clarity:** Decision-makers at all levels need clear signals that will help them decide what action they should take. Comprehensive information buries signals in noise; information should be selective. Therefore, it is important to select aspects of ecosystem well-being, people-ecosystem interactions, and human well-being that:

— most reveal improvements or declines in these conditions and interactions; and
— are relevant, appropriate and clear to the decision-makers concerned.

If the people making the assessment and the decision-makers using the assessment are one and the same, this is not likely to be a problem. If they are different, special care will be needed to fulfill these requirements. It is therefore important to ask:

— Who is doing the assessment?
— Who can use the assessment?
— How do the two communicate?
— Are both committed to continuous assessment?
— Are the decision-makers concerned committed to act on information gained through the assessment?

Communicating assessments

Assessments should be communicated in whichever ways are most useful and meaningful to the decision-makers concerned. This includes:

• Starting by identifying the full range of decision-makers concerned. For example, a community that is weakened by the policies of central government would want the findings of its assessment to be communicated to decision-makers in central government and those who influence them.

- If necessary, communicating the assessment in different ways to different groups of decision-makers and other users: different products and events (not necessarily reports); and communication in different media.
- Using the right jargon for each group of users. Jargon tends to have a poor reputation. However, communication that tries to avoid it can end up being unintelligible (or simply boring) to its intended audience.
- Giving feedback (in a useful form) to people who provide information for the assessment.

Often the most useful task that an assessment can do is expose unsolved problems and identify untapped solutions. Such information is most likely to be obtained by processes that reward the constructive identification of failure. In turn, solutions are most likely to be implemented if the decision-makers concerned perceive them as reasonable, respectable and recognizable.

Conclusion

Monitoring and evaluating strategy performance has been one of the least developed elements of the strategy process. It is also one of the most important. Mechanisms need to be set in place so that nations or communities can steer their development according to the benefits of experience, and with the knowledge of changing circumstances, so that it stays on a sustain-

able path. This is not easy, for it requires the nation or community to have a practical vision of sustainability expressed in its own terms. That vision will have a strong ethical and qualitative basis which has rarely been well-defined. How can a strategy assess its progress and course against goals that are intangible?

Usually, conventional methods of monitoring and evaluation rely on physical, economic or social indicators to measure what was achieved in the past, at either national or project level. These often focus on input supplies and their immediate results, especially at the project level. They might consider the number of hospital beds in a country or the number of trees planted in a village. The emphasis has been on measuring past performance through tangible products, and then considering what implications this has for future performance. These methods will continue to be valuable, although more emphasis is needed on those underlying, less tangible qualities of development which lead to sustainability.

The experience so far has been sparse, but three directions for change are emerging:

1.	Emphasis needs to be on indices governing the way things are done rather than what has been done.

2.	In an environment of change and uncertainty, the concern should be primarily on modifying and influencing future performance and not on evaluating the past. The key to developing appropriate appraisal methods is understanding strategies in terms of constant change and adaptation to future needs.

3.   These methods must themselves be ingredients of sustainable development and not something external to it. Concepts of action research or monitoring through action are appropriate here. They imply that those people involved in managing the strategy process, and in all elements of implementation, are each involved in a feedback loop of action–reflection–reaction. This works best at the local level where the reflection and feedback terms are more immediately beneficial to the participants.

As a consequence, assessment of strategies, including monitoring, evaluation and reporting, needs to stress process as well as products, and be anticipatory and action-based.

PART 3

Resources to Drive
the Strategy

Chapter 10

Financing Strategies and the Role of External Agencies

Funding agencies have played a crucial role in the development of national strategies, and there are many ways to make the most of their involvement. There is a pressing need for donor coordination, so that the capacities of recipient communities are not undermined or distracted by overlapping and sometimes conflicting demands. There has been a tendency for donors to pick and choose from a portfolio of proposed actions, with the result that the strategy loses its importance as an overall framework for sustainable development. Also, donor support has been patchy, both in terms of the range of actions supported and continuity. Defining approaches for greater financial security needs to be given high priority.

National Environment Funds (NEFs) can contribute to long-term stable financing for strategies. Because NEFs rely on participatory management approaches, they also engender greater local control and self-reliance. One of the most attractive features of an NEF is its ability to distribute its funding consistently over a long period at levels which local institutions can effectively absorb.

Like external funding, technical assistance to national strategies from international organizations has had mixed results. There are important lessons on how to involve expatriate personnel. Experience has shown that international NGOs, in particular, can continue to play a vital role in providing the appropriate kinds of technical support to strategy teams.

No matter how successful some national strategies have been in attracting funds for their planning and implementation, the levels of resources are insignificant when compared to those associated with the big forces shaping development, such as structural adjustment policies and World Bank loans. For the remainder of the decade, the most important task for NSDSs will be to harness and modify those forces to be consistent with local sustainable development goals.

The role of donors

In many lower-income countries, support from bilateral, multi-lateral and financial organizations is often necessary for the development and implementation of a strategy. Also, many donors consider a strategy to be an effective means of ensuring that their support is well-targeted and is applied within a locally-defined policy framework. It is recognized that strategies are a way of improving and integrating social, economic and environmental policies, and building national capacities to develop and implement such policies. But they can fulfill this role only if they are nationally-driven, participatory processes, and this takes time.

It is important to ensure that both national and external expectations and perceptions of the purpose of a strategy are consistent and mutually supportive. The wrong kinds of external support can lead to insufficient internalization of strategies and a concomitant lack of government commitment and loss of momentum. They may also result in irrelevant or damaging activities. If donors treat strategies merely as assessments, documents or plans, for example, they may be completed quickly, but they will no longer be strategies and their results will be trivial: a report and a few projects.

Concern about the role of donors as manipulators of national and local strategies, rather than as facilitators, has come to a head for two reasons. First, there is a growing number of cases where a multiplicity of donors support different initiatives in countries which have little capacity to coordinate them. Second, environmental conditions are being tied to the receipt of grants and loans.

The problem of too many players has sometimes led to more money than can be absorbed, a glut of expatriate consultants, and activities run by staff with salaries and resources which set them apart from the institutions with which they are trying to work. Donors can be a creative force, stimulating governments and communities to rethink options and ways of managing change. But they need to work in a way that is appropriate to local conditions, and build upon existing initiatives. Recent guidelines by donors on ensuring the sustainability of their development assistance are to be welcomed (for example, SDC 1991). Donors' investments in strategies should lead to greater self-reliance and autonomy in the communities concerned; this will require a thorough review of existing investment patterns and an emphasis on options for sustainable financing.

Donor coordination

The donor community should be considered as participants in the strategy from the very beginning of the process. Yet the principal lesson for donors – underlying all others – is that strategies must be led by the

Box 24: Ten lessons for donors

These are the ten main lessons for donors (for simplicity, both development assistance agencies and lending institutions/banks are here called donors), which have been learned through more than ten years of their involvement in strategies.

1. Coordinate donor activities: Recipient governments must be supported in taking a leading role in coordinating external contributions to the strategy process.

2. Invest in the long-term: Low-level continuous external backing over a long period is almost always much better than short, high-level, one-off inputs (unless contributing to a strategy trust fund).

3. Support the process: Programme funding is needed for the capacity-building process; not just the products of strategic planning. Programme-oriented approaches are often more valuable than projects that are not an integral part of a strategy.

4. Support existing strategies: If funding is conditional, the conditions should respect alternative approaches to strategies that exist locally. Buy in to existing processes, even if they do not quite fit the bill.

5. Do not impose external models: The corollary to supporting 'homemade' or tailor-made strategies is the need to guard against designing for schedules, budgets and skills which do not fit with local norms and capacities.

6. Form and encourage partnerships: Close working links with other donors and partnerships, and support for a variety of participants in a strategy, both governmental and non-governmental, add momentum and stability to the process. A good first step is to help governments identify stakeholders and their potential contributions.

7. Seek coherence in aid programmes: Each donor needs to ensure that all components of its support interrelate and build upon each other within the strategy process.

8. Devise new forms of assessment: Donors need to develop new indicators for sustainability and evaluation to reflect and give greater importance to the qualitative and process elements of strategies.

9. Refocus existing investment: Donors need to review all elements of their aid programmes and help governments refocus existing investments towards sustainable development principles and objectives defined through the strategy process. This refocusing will be more important than initiating new 'environment' projects.

10. Be flexible and creative in financial arrangements: Support innovative financing mechanisms; for example, National Environment Funds, which lead to consistency and self-reliance in maintaining the strategy process.

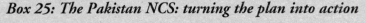

Box 25: The Pakistan NCS: turning the plan into action

The following exercise was used in Pakistan by a technical working group supporting the multi-donor group for NCS implementation. Using wall charts, three levels of information were set out:

1. The recommended strategy programmes and actions and their rationale were set out in the top row.
2. Current programmes, projects and activities under each of the recommended strategy programmes were set out in the second row. Programmes and projects that fell roughly into the NCS programme area were included, and any part of the programme that did not meet, or conflicted with, NCS objectives was noted.
3. The commitments and disbursements by donors and lenders in each of the programme areas were set out in the bottom row.

Information for this exercise came from the UNDP computer database for the Development Cooperation Report, which documents in detail most donor-supported projects in lower-income countries. Information was requested on all current public sector investments by donors in programmes and projects that fell under the recommended strategy programmes.

Although the data on commitments and disbursements were not exactly quantifiable, they gave information that was critical for NCS implementation, such as:

- a clear indication of areas of shortfall in donor support to programmes recommended in the NCS document;
- an indication of where there was heavy donor investment in programmes that were producing obviously harmful environmental effects (such as large-scale expansion of irrigation and chemically-intensive agriculture) — these were flagged for refocusing, or for the addition of an environmental management component; and
- an indication of the absorptive capacity of the programme area, and hence, where emphasis should be put on refocusing measures and building capacity.

recipient country. This applies particularly to the coordination of donor participation. The increasing influence of external forces, often operating at the same time within a country but supporting different and uncoordinated strategy initiatives, has led to considerable bewilderment in many developing countries. It has caused a diversion of existing capacity and an undermining of local initiative. It has resulted in a substantial waste of international and national resources and, all too frequently, a loss of momentum in aspects of environmental policy to which governments were already committed.

Yet, in order for governments to take the lead in donor coordination, they require considerable resources and a firm commitment to cooperate by the external agencies. Permanent coordinating mechanisms are often lacking. In some countries, UNDP has taken the lead in coordination; in the case of NEAPs, the World Bank has led. Donors frequently have an interest in meeting independently from government when defining the focal areas for their assistance, or when wishing to develop common positions on what they feel to be an important issue of principle. While this interaction between the external players is important and should be encouraged, ultimately the government must be supported to exercise the leadership role in coordination.

Experience suggests a number of key ingredients for successful donor coordination:

- The government could empower a central ministry with authority to establish coordination mechanisms and procedures. This ministry may be the strategy secretariat, but might more usefully be the official contact point for donors, such as the Ministry of Foreign Affairs or Finance. In some cases, the national planning authority, with its cross-sectoral functions, might be the best choice.
- Coordination activities often require

special skills of synthesis and facilitation. Donors should make sure that coordination is not undermined by a lack of the necessary capacities.
- Local NGOs and private sector representatives also need to be brought into the donor coordination process at regular intervals.
- Effective coordination depends greatly on improved information exchange among donors on their investment portfolios and policies, including evaluation reports and other analyses of the country situation.
- Donors should seek to minimize and simplify their interventions so that coordination by government is less onerous. In-country missions, for example, should be limited in size and number, jointly undertaken, and scheduled so that the unnecessary impact on government business is reduced.

The early formation of a donor coordination group, and regular briefings, can help to achieve understanding of the purpose and the implications of a strategy. It will also foster the cohesion among the donor community necessary to ensure sustained and coherent support for the strategy.

In Pakistan, the government established a multi-donor coordination group specifically to integrate donor support for NCS implementation. A special technical working group was established to assist the donors; methods used are summarized in Box 25.

Strategy cohesion

An important aspect of donor coordination is division of financial assistance according to the sectoral preferences of the donors. This issue needs to be addressed early on. At the same time, donors should take care to ensure that dividing assistance by sectors does not reduce the cohesion of the overall strategy. Donors should integrate their aid or lending programmes into the priorities set by the strategy. Regardless of the preferences of donors, support is needed for the process, and for priority sectors as determined through the strategy.

Donor interests and the availability of financial support should not deflect strategies from their planned strategic focus. Definition of 'bankable' projects should be undertaken as part of the strategy and not dominate or be separated from the process. Donors have specific needs; for example, a portfolio of fundable projects, ordered according to clear priorities that have been established as part of a strategic process. Such needs should be stated clearly at the outset. The donors and lending agencies should work with the partner government so that these needs can be met as part of the process, without otherwise influencing its design or timetable. In other words, the portfolio of projects would be one of the intended products of the strategy process. But it would be up to the government and other national participants in the strategy to decide on the objectives of the strategy, the design and timetable of the process, how it would be managed, when it would produce the portfolio of projects, and what the projects would be.

Failure to uncouple the particular needs of donors from the overall design and management of the strategy has damaged some strategies. In some cases, the timetable of the process has been compressed to produce a portfolio of projects as quickly as possible; usually too quickly for a coherent strategy to be developed in a participatory manner. In other cases, the donor has simply ignored the strategy, insisting that a new 'strategy' be prepared to draw up the portfolio of projects.

During implementation, there is a great danger of slipping back into a project approach, making it more difficult for the country to retain control of its strategy. Big projects can quickly distort or sidetrack the strategy process. A special effort should be made by both the strategy secretariat and donors to maintain the strategic or programme focus of the strategy while recognizing the project basis of donor funding.

Funding security

A broad base of donor support is likely to be most effective. A strategy can be expected to include a wide range of activities involving the government, corporate sector, NGOs and communities. It is unlikely that any one donor will be able to sustain long-term support for all such activities. Thus, setting out to capture the interest of the larger donor community will be most desirable.

Broad support brings greater:

- resilience;
- coverage;
- confidence; and
- continuity.

The earlier in the strategy a donor consortium can be formed to support it, the better.

To promote NEAPs, the World Bank has tended to initiate discussions with governments by guaranteeing start-up funds. At the same time, through round table and one-to-one meetings, the Bank seeks other partners in the process among the bilateral donors and, more recently, UNDP. USAID is the principal donor in the Uganda NEAP, for example. In Zambia, the World Bank and UNDP shared the cost of the NEAP. Engaging a bilateral donor early in the process increases the chances of continuity and support following the preparation of an action plan and project portfolio. To date, the Bank has not contributed grant funds beyond the first phase in an NEAP; any substantial contributions to NEAP implementation are expected to come from a range of donors picking up individual projects or through Bank sector loans. It is too early in the history of NEAPs to determine the extent to which they will become perma-

nently integrated within government and continue with or without external support.

The history of NCSs and other independently initiated strategies has shown that, without this initial guarantee of start-up funds, many have never gone beyond a good idea. Others stalled when an individual donor supporting the planning phase did not continue funding for implementation. The World Bank has never contributed to a non-NEAP strategy, even in cases where it has accepted an existing process as satisfying NEAP requirements.

Loss of external support has not always meant the end of a strategy process. In fact, where the initial external contributions were modest, with the greater proportion of cost shouldered by local institutions, this has rarely been the case. A key to successful donor participation lies in understanding the absorptive capacity over time of the local administration or community undertaking the strategy. In most cases, small-scale, continuous, external backing over a long period is much better than short, high-level, one-off or irregular external inputs.

Priority needs to be given to supporting a core strategy process which provides the principal energy source for stimulating and maintaining action throughout the system. In the past, long-term commitments have not been easy when donors were locked into a project and not a process orientation. Yet a number of bilateral aid agencies, such as the

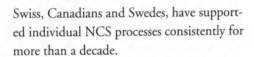

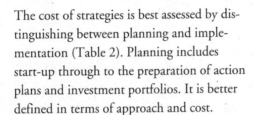

Swiss, Canadians and Swedes, have supported individual NCS processes consistently for more than a decade.

The cost of strategies

The cost of strategies is best assessed by distinguishing between planning and implementation (Table 2). Planning includes start-up through to the preparation of action plans and investment portfolios. It is better defined in terms of approach and cost.

The planning phase for NCSs has lasted anywhere from two to six years and has usually included a range of demonstration and capacity-building programmes. NCSs which were prepared through local initiative, such as those in Zimbabwe and Nigeria, cost very little and were undertaken within existing government budgets. In Costa Rica, the NCS document took three years to prepare, at a cost of US$220,000, of which 50 per cent came from six different external agencies, and 50 per cent from the

Table 2: Cost of selected strategies

	Cost US$mil	Period	Donor
Strategy planning			
Costa Rica NCS	0.22	1987–89	50% IUCN, CI, WWF US, TNC, 50% national
Ethiopia NCS	1.60	1989–94	SIDA, ODA, NORAD, UNSO
Guinea NEAP	0.65	1990–91	WB, CIDA, UNDP, USAID, FAO, UNEP, UNSO
Zambia NCS	0.60	1984–88	SIDA, Dutch, CIDA
Zambia NEAP	1.00	1994–95	WB, UNDP
Kenya NEAP	2.20	1994–95	WB
Uganda NEAP	1.00	1991–94	USAID, WB, SIDA, UNSO, UNDP
Nepal NCS	0.50	1982–88	SIDA, SDC, USAID, CIDA, WWF
Nepal NEPAP	0.03	1993	Ford Foundation, IUCN
Pakistan NCS	2.60	1988–93	CIDA
Strategy implementation			
Nepal NCS	3.50	1989–94	SDC, UNICEF, USAID
Seychelles NEMP	50.00	1992–96	Various
Colombia NEP	972.00	1990–94	60% national, 40% various
Zambia NEAP	2.00	1994–97	Dutch
Madagascar NEAP	85.00	1990–95	SDC, USAID, WB, UNDP, NORAD, ADB

government's Ministry of Natural Resources. The Pakistan NCS cost US$2.6 million over five years and was funded entirely by CIDA.

In general, NEAPs have tended to be more expensive and prepared in less time. In Africa, NEAPs have usually taken an average of 18 months to prepare, and have cost anywhere from US$300,000 to US$3 million. Major donors supporting NEAP preparation have been the World Bank, UNDP, UNSO, and USAID. NCSs have been supported by a broader range of bilateral donors than have NEAPs, although more recently a number of countries, such as Norway, Japan, France and Sweden, have provided bilateral funding for specific NEAP activities, sometimes through the Bank. NEAP preparation has not usually included the same level of implementation activities as the NCS planning phases. The experience with NCSs worldwide has been fairly consistent, while for NEAPs the approach has varied greatly from region to region. In Nepal, for example, at Bank instigation, a National Environment Policy and Action Plan costing US$30,000 was prepared over six months as part of the NCS process.

The cost of implementing strategies varies greatly depending on the coverage of the action plan. The initial phase of the Nepal NCS implementation programme was limited to cross-sectoral demonstration activities. It focused on setting in place the key elements of a future environmental management framework for the government. The programme has cost about US$1 million each year. On the other hand, external support to the various sectoral master plans that fall within the NCS umbrella have attracted several hundred millions of dollars. The investment portfolio designed for the Seychelles National Environment Management Plan defines US$50 million in project concepts, from conventional protected area initiatives to sewage and pollution control programmes. Colombia has defined a five-year National Environment Programme ending in 1994, costing US$972 million. Only about US$200 million of this has been raised; 60 per cent from national government budgets and the remainder from external sources including the Ecological Coffee Fund, TFAP, debt-for-nature swaps and soft loans for environmental infrastructure. Colombia was attempting to allocate 0.55 per cent of its GNP to sustainable management of natural resources.

The advantage of a comprehensive investment portfolio is that the external and internal agencies participating in the scheme begin to see the links between their activities within the strategy framework. The disadvantage is that rarely are all projects funded, so that, for all practical purposes, the strategy disintegrates into bits and pieces. It is probably better to limit the size of a strategy implementation programme to well-targeted activities that reinforce the strategy.

Box 26: *National environment funds*

A National Environment Fund is a publicly or privately constituted organization which solicits and manages funds from various sources and makes grants to support environmental and sustainable development projects. A trust arrangement is common. Most national funds are created and managed through a participatory process that involves different sectors of society, government, non-governmental organizations, academics, and others in designing the institution or project grant criteria.

If properly designed and operated, NEFs can be the catalyst to improve environmental management, biodiversity conservation, and sustainable and equitable use of resources.

NEFs can be set up as endowments or pass-through grant-making facilities. They can be funded through a variety of mechanisms such as debt-for-nature swaps, debt for-giveness schemes, in-country fees on tourism, and direct contributions from donors. They can be one unitary fund or a structure incorporating multiple sub-accounts.

NEFs can include various attributes which make them attractive for funding sustainable development:

- **Support of national strategies:** NEFs can ensure that national environmental planning frameworks are effective tools for ordering national priorities rather than being simply prerequisites for donor assistance. They do this by putting the environmental action plans on a stable financial footing and ensuring that selected priorities represent a consensus of relevant players.
- **Stable financing:** NEFs have the potential to provide the stable long-term financing necessary for the effective implementation of conservation actions.
- **Appropriate scale:** NEFs provide an institutional mechanism for disbursing appropriately-sized funds that are within the capacities of beneficiary institutions to effectively absorb.
- **Participation:** NEFs encourage the participation of a wide range of interested parties; for example, through representation on boards of directors, technical review committees, and general assemblies.
- **Transparency:** Decision-making in the NEFs is subject to public review and critique.
- **Cooperation:** NEFs promote democratic values of participation, cooperation and accountability, which have implications beyond the environmental sector.
- **Strategy cohesion:** NEFs help nurture the growth of trained national personnel and avoid uneven coverage of environmental priorities.

box continues

- **Balanced priorities:** NEFs offer a promising means for balancing global priorities with national needs and aspirations. This occurs in the negotiation over criteria for the management of sub-accounts set up by particular donors.
- **Donor Coordination:** NEFs can play an important role in donor coordination by providing a focal point for negotiation (especially regarding the need to link in with existing strategies), accounting, monitoring, evaluation and auditing.

A particularly important component of an implementation programme, which should be given high priority for funding, is the development of methods for reviewing and refocusing conventional areas of government and private sector investment in resource development. Approaches include various forms of environmental assessment and audit and a reorientation by donors of their investment in the main resource management sectors to emphasize sustainable use and environment protection.

National environment funds

New methods and structures which promote self-reliance and local control are needed for funding strategies. One of the most promising approaches is the design of national environment funds (NEF) so that they can become a core source of finance for strategy implementation. The NEF concept was first tested in 1990 as a means of distributing funds generated through debt-for-nature swaps. NEFs have since expanded in their scope to cover a wide range of sustainable development activities. There are now funds operating or planned in more than 20 countries in Asia, Africa and Latin America (Table 3). More than US$290 million has been committed to these funds and more than 100 projects have already been funded. The main characteristics of NEFs are summarized in Box 26, with case studies of funds operating in Bolivia and Colombia shown in boxes 27 and 28.

The most attractive aspect of the NEF approach is that it is consistent with the most important principles of the strategy process, such as encouraging broad participation, openness and accountability. At the same time it counters some of the key weaknesses of strategies by providing a consistent long-term source of funding under a flexible management regime that can be adapted to best suit local requirements.

Another weakness of strategies has been their failure to engage people who understand and work with finances. Binding NEFs into national strategies will bring together skills to attract, manage and disperse funds. Most important, strategy teams

Table 3: Overview of some national environment funds

Country/name of fund	$ committed (millions)	Source of funding	Year
Asia			
Bhutan / Bhutan Trust for Environmental Conservation	12.6	GEF, Dutch, WWF, Norway	91–2
Philippines / Foundation for the Philippine Environment	25.4	USAID Debt Swap, Bank of Tokyo Debt Swap, USAID Debt Swap	90–2
Indonesia	20.0	USAID	90
Africa			
Madagascar	12.0	GEF	92
Uganda	4.0	GEF	93
Latin America and the Caribbean			
Argentina	3.1	EAI	93
Bolivia / FONAMA	80.3	EAI, GEF, WB, IADB, USAID/ PL-480, TNC Debt Swap, WWF-Debt Swap, Govt of Bolivia Debt Swap, US Govt, Japan, Switzerland, Canada, Sweden, Mexico, Germany, Holland	91
Colombia / ECOFONDO	58.5	EAI, Canada, USAID/IUCN/TNC, WWF	92–3
Chile	18.7	EAI	91
Dominican Republic / PRONATURA	0.6	Puerto Rico Conservation Trust	91
El Salvador / SEMA	49.2	EAI, Canada	92–3
Guatemala / Guatemala Trust for Environmental Conservation	0.8	UK Foundation, WWF, US banks	92
Honduras / Fundación VIDA	7.0	Govt Bond-debt forgiveness, USAID	92–3
Jamaica / Environmental Foundation of Jamaica	22.0	USAID and PR Conservation Trust	91
Jamaica Conservation and Development Trust	0.7	TNC, Eagle Commercial Bank	91–2
Mexico / Fondo Mexicano para la Conservación de la Naturaleza	20.2	US State Dept, USAID, Bankers Trust, MacArthur Foundation, WWF, USAID	93
Panama / Fundación NATURA	25.8	USAID, TNC, Panama	91
Peru / PROFONANPE	5.5	GTZ, GE	93
Uruguay	7.0	EAI	92

would include resident staff who have the skills to use the NEF as a lever for attracting national contributions over time. Money in the bank builds confidence and is an incentive for cooperation. Governments will usually contribute on a regular basis under these conditions.

Developing an NEF

The process of developing a NEF can take more than two years. It involves negotiations with different constituent groups and with donors. There are several key steps:

- an interim advisory board is selected with representatives from diverse sectors involved in the national strategy;
- consultation is carried out with the different sectors in all regions of the country to receive advice on appropriate goals, management practices and grant criteria for the fund;
- the board defines the terms of reference for the fund's staff, the appropriate legal constitution and a charter and bylaws;
- the charter and bylaws that contain the purpose and restrictions of the fund, as well as its management structure, need to be discussed and finalized in consultation with the main strategy constituents and potential donors; and
- a permanent board is elected, staff are hired and, once funding is secured, an NEF can commence soliciting proposals and making grants.

Disadvantages of NEFs

Already, in the short experience with NEFs, there are pitfalls that some funds have encountered, such as:

- Governments can use the existence of a fund to avoid addressing their wider responsibilities;
- Funds should not implement projects, so as to avoid competing with their clients.
- The first donors to support a fund often have sought to control its decisions and operation, deterring other potential donors who view it as claimed territory.

Each of these problems can be avoided with thorough consultation and flexibility by the strategy team. They need to adjust the fund design to accommodate the needs of various constituents, while pointing out to them the experiences of funds elsewhere in the world.

NEFs should seek to cover some of the costs of a strategy's core implementation activities and support a wide range of projects that tackle high-priority issues or are useful for catalytic or demonstration functions. It is unlikely that a fund will cover the bulk of strategy investment required. In the former Eastern Bloc countries, for example, environmental funds are a popular mechanism for contributing to pollution clean-up costs. Yet, in the Slovak Republic, for instance, it is estimated that the cost of meeting the country's environmental objectives would require 50 per cent of GNP, while the

Box 27: Bolivia's NEF

Bolivia's NEF, FONAMA (Fondo Nacional para el Medio Ambiente), is a flexible independent public institution housed in the Bolivian government. One of the oldest and most fully-developed of all NEFs, FONAMA started in 1990 as a mechanism for the management of debt-for-nature swaps. Its first effort was to promote commercial and bilateral debt swaps to support conservation and sustainable development projects. Its role expanded to include raising and managing funds from various sources for investment in conservation, sustainable development, and environmental quality. FONAMA is now responsible for organizing all investments in the environment in Bolivia, seeking to integrate government activities with those of indigenous communities and NGOs. It is governed by a board that includes representatives of the government, NGOs and the private sector, and is assisted by an administrative council that provides both technical and administrative support and is responsible for fund raising.

FONAMA is an umbrella structure composed of two main parts: an Enterprise of the Americas Initiative account, and a World Bank/Global Environmental Facility/Government of Switzerland account. It also includes at least 16 sub-accounts of various sizes, each with different characteristics, objectives, and management structures, as determined by the source and purposes of the funds obtained.

To date, FONAMA has secured commitments (both actual transfers and legally binding obligations) of just over US$47 million and claims additional pledges of US$33 million that are being negotiated. As of mid-1993, FONAMA had approved 44 projects, ranging in size from US$11,000 to US$13 million, with a total value of US$27 million. These were in various stages of execution, including US$2 million worth of projects which had been completed.

government's contribution to the fund is less than 2 per cent of GNP. Strategy teams will need to continually explore other creative ways of maintaining funding commitments to the process.

NEFs are also attractive for donors. They provide donors with the facility to move large sums of money cheaply. NEFs can be a wholesale disbursement facility while achieving other donor objectives inherent in the national strategy process. Also, having a team of finance professionals working for sustainable development means that funds can be managed in a way which satisfies donors, with separate accounts and governing structures if necessary.

The role of international NGOs and expatriates

'Technical teams are transitory. Communities are permanent.'

Dionisio Batista, IUCN Panama

It is most important to use nationals of the country as much as possible, to rely on national capacities, and to build national capacities where they are lacking. Expatriate personnel should assist only where local expertise is lacking. Donors and other external agencies should not supply an expatriate team to run the strategy process for the country; nor should expatriates dominate the team. Expatriates must possess experience and qualifications not found locally, and should have an understanding of local political, socio-cultural, economic and other issues. Ideally, they should also be able to communicate in the local language.

Advantages

The advantages of expatriate involvement can include the following:

- they can bring new ideas;
- they can work synergistically with local experience;
- they provide strong links with donors, enabling projects to be picked up much faster;
- they have stronger links to top-level decision-makers, who may accept expatriates' recommendations more readily (not always the case, nor always an advantage); and
- they provide training and capacity-building.

Disadvantages

The disadvantages might include:

- expatriates pick the brains of local experts (who often receive no credit or financial benefit), leading to animosity;
- some expatriates lack necessary expertise;
- expatriate ideas and perceptions are often not attuned to local circumstances, and are therefore impractical;
- expatriates may not be as good as local people at assessing local situations;
- they have a lack of commitment to implementation and continuity in short-term assignments; and
- their salaries and benefits are a sensitive issue since, generally, they are higher than local rates.

Remuneration and allowances for local staff and local consultants should be set by the host country, not by the donors, after cross-sectoral discussion and agreement. This will avoid large disparities between project staff and their peers in government service.

International NGOs

The OECD (1987) has pointed out that international NGOs, in their own right,

Box 28: Colombia's NEF

Colombia's NEF, *ECOFONDO*, was initiated as a multi-purpose, private, non-profit trust fund to allocate resources for the environment. Initially, funding was to be provided by a rebate of the 4 per cent import tax on Colombian coffee into Europe: although the proposal ultimately proved to be unworkable, the idea of the fund endured. A participatory process was developed, involving both government and NGOs. In early 1993, the core group of organizers convened a constitutional assembly for what is now called the *ECOFONDO*. At that time, 110 NGOs signed an enabling declaration as founding members of the fund, and the possibility is open for the involvement of environmental NGOs that are not founding members.

As of May 1993, 270 NGOs and 18 government agencies had expressed an interest in being members of the future Corporación ECOFONDO. Its structure includes a general assembly to allow full representation of all interested groups and a large potential number of regional committees. It has a board of directors involving both government and NGOs, technical committees to help with the evaluation and selection of projects, and regional advisory boards for each of the 12 major regions of Colombia. It also includes an Office of the Executive Director and an independent auditor.

In July 1993, ECOFONDO was granted full legal status. It is intended to operate as an endowed fund, although there are no restrictions against use of the principal funds. The current plan is for early infusions of funds to be used primarily for projects, while subsequent monies will be allocated increasingly towards an endowment.

One of the first tasks of *ECOFONDO* is to manage funds derived from the Enterprise for the Americas debt reduction. Through this programme, it expects to receive approximately US$38 million over the next 10 years. As of August 1993, an *ECOFONDO* account had already received close to US$6 million in local currency. *ECOFONDO* has also reached an agreement with the Canadian government to set up a sub-account with another $13 million from renegotiation of Canadian bilateral debt. This programme was announced by Canada at UNCED in 1992.

make a significant contribution to funding for development assistance (about 10 per cent of the level of official development assistance worldwide). It has noted a number of positive features about international NGO assistance that are pertinent to their participation in national strategies, whatever their funding sources:

- much of their help is either through, or in cooperation with, local community groups;
- they tend to concentrate their activities in the least developed countries;
- they tend to direct their assistance towards the poor and other disadvantaged groups;
- they often provide a presence in rural areas or in neglected parts of urban communities and emphasize self-help approaches;
- they can work effectively with local or regional governments;
- they are often well-positioned and inclined to try out new ideas or techniques; and
- they use experts who tend to be committed to community-based work, and who often cost less because of a willingness to live closer to local people.

Donors need to give much greater emphasis to supporting the role of international NGOs in national strategies. When compared with international consulting companies, NGOs often bring a longer-term commitment to the countries they are serving, greater flexibility, and better value for money. Large organizations like UNDP and the World Bank need to form partnerships with international NGOs which can work on a scale, and with a form of intimate involvement, that brings the best results

when technical support is requested by national strategy teams. The use by these big donors of large expatriate missions, involving ad hoc consultants can be especially counter-productive and can drain local capacities when more sensitive inputs would better encourage local initiative and action.

International NGOs can also help donors to identify and remove international barriers to the implementation of national strategies. Such barriers include: externally-determined development aid, unfavourable trade conditions, debt, and structural adjustment policies that do not support the national strategy.

Conclusion

There are three issues of special importance to the financial security of strategies for sustainable development and to the future role of international organizations.

1. Innovative and flexible financial arrangements. These can bring greater local control and security to the strategy process. There are various forms of trusts or endowments which work on a consistent level of return through interest on a principal sum. Also, grant funding can be particularly useful in the early years of a strategy. These need to be tested more widely, particularly in the least developed countries where government budgets and capacities are constrained through structural adjustments. Donors will need to invest in the process of discussion and design leading to the most appropriate form of fund for local conditions, whether government-run, private, or a mix of the two. In some cases, it is better to create an NGO-dominated fund, focusing on support to smaller scale activities, so that government commitment to internalizing investment for environment protection is not diminished.

Although NEFs are an important way to organize and coordinate external funding in a country, ultimately they must aim to mobilize national resources. They should explore, for example, ways of channelling taxes, charges or fines associated with the use of natural resources or maintenance of environmental quality to the fund.

Biodiversity-rich but economically-poor countries might consider special visa charges for tourists, as a form of biodiversity rental that would replenish the fund instead of a consolidated revenue account. Pollution fines, park entry fees, and various charges for the use of what may previously have been free environmental goods might also go to the fund.

In countries such as Vietnam, where the private sector is becoming the main force for development in a largely unregulated system, special methods are needed to encourage contributions from large and externally-financed development, while giving emphasis to helping small local enterprises define sustainable use strategies.

Creative financing options such as these should move away from dependency in strategy implementation and build a local sense of environmental responsibility and ownership.

2. Analysis of the sustainability of existing development investment. The current approach to national strategies, encouraged through the World Bank-promoted NEAPs, is to define a portfolio of environment-related projects which are then marketed to donors.

This approach has a number of problems, the most important being that it can divert attention from a more detailed assessment of how existing government and donor budgets are allocated. A US$3 million environment project, for example, becomes insignificant when applied in an area where US$100 million investments are supporting larger schemes.

A priority in strategy implementation needs to be applying forms of environmental or sustainable use assessment to the major development financing so that modifications, adjustments and reallocations can be made consistent with strategy objectives. Otherwise, the impacts of specific environmental projects will be insignificant in terms of the mainstream of development. Sustainability analysis might include:

- comprehensive regional reviews followed by investment programmes, such as those now being developed for the Ethiopian NCS through an extensive consultative process within the framework;

- various forms of environmental auditing, for example, the procedures governing industry performance within the European Community; and
- a green reporting process as introduced recently in Norway.

The Norwegian initiative is particularly important in demonstrating the continuing role for a central strategy agency in monitoring the effectiveness of strategy implementation. In Norway, each sectoral agency is required to report in detail on how its budget is allocated to achieve sustainable development goals. If, in successive years, the strategy agency (in this case the environment ministry) considers that a sector has failed to live up to its targets, then the agency can recommend to parliament that the associated budget is reallocated to other programmes which are performing better within or outside the sector.

3. Awareness of the forces shaping development. In the least developed countries, for example, these forces include the terms of international trade under the General Agreement on Tariffs and Trade (GATT), structural adjustment policies required by the IMF and the overall economic philosophy and loan policy pursued by the World Bank. There has been a tendency for participants to be ignorant or unaware of the importance of these forces

which means, inevitably, that the process is overrun by them.

A principal aim of the framework for trade and the policies of these organizations is to encourage export-oriented integration of developing countries in the world economy. Such policies are driven by economic values. Balancing those values with the other objectives of sustainable development needs to be a central concern of international and national strategy processes in both the developed and developing worlds.

Increasing economic links between countries creates complex environmental relationships, which will need to be accounted for in terms of trade and aid. Special commodity-related environmental agreements between two countries or blocks of countries will be needed, so as to address the environmental impacts embodied in a country's imports and exports of goods and services.

Donor countries must begin to more effectively match their aid policies with analysis of the environmental debts (and importation of carrying capacity) that may be hidden in their relationship with recipients. If Western consumption patterns encourage the production of (for example) bananas in Costa Rica or carpets in Nepal, then the aid programmes of importing countries need to help address the significant environmental externalities associated with these products. Relying simply on the producing country to apply the Polluter

Pays Principle, when the necessary capacities are lacking, can worsen inequities and ruin local community economies. Special policies and phased programmes of support to the industries concerned may be needed and should be built in to the national strategies of both the donor and recipient countries.

Structural adjustment involves major injections of external funds into the economy of a country (on highly concessional terms) on the understanding that certain changes will be made in how the economy is managed. Usually, these changes involve trimming back the public sector, reducing or eliminating subsidies, greatly increased emphasis on private investment and giving priority to increasing export earnings.

Structural adjustment policies could be designed to achieve sustainable development objectives but, to date, the process has not been oriented in this way, nor has it included mechanisms to integrate environmental concerns. On the contrary, the Asian Development Bank has found that structural adjustment policies in a number of countries in its region may have led to environmental degradation (ADB, 1990).

Strategy teams will need to forge partnerships and acquire the technical expertise and methods which will allow them to incorporate these complex effects of structural adjustment policies and associated loans. The IMF and the World Bank will need to give increasing resources to assisting in this process and to tailoring policies that reinforce, and not undermine, environment goals.

Creative responses will be needed. Given the net flow of funds from South to North due to the servicing of debt over the past decade, loans for environment protection and sustainable development may continue to create as many problems as they solve. Greater emphasis on debt relief in exchange for various environmental services, such as the conservation of biodiversity, is an important option.

National sustainable development strategies provide an opportunity to expose many of the inequities and imbalances that result from economic policies and past trading relationships among countries. More importantly, they provide an opportunity to introduce mechanisms for correcting these imbalances.

References

The ideas and information which led to this handbook were drawn mainly from the regional networks of people with experience in strategies who have been coming together regularly over the past two years in Africa, Asia and Latin America. Some of the written products of their work appear in this list. We have not attempted to compile a comprehensive bibliography of reports and papers on strategies. Instead, we have only identified those key policy statements by various organizations or governments which relate to strategies and which themselves provide more detailed reference material. These were the primary sources for the handbook. They include the main global policy documents, such as the World Conservation Strategy, Caring for the Earth and Agenda 21, as well as some more specific sources cited within the text, from which examples have been taken.

The World Resources Institute (WRI), in collaboration with IUCN and IIED, regularly produce comprehensive directories of strategy documents which are available from any of the three organizations.

ADB (1990) *Economic Policies for Sustainable Development.* ADB, Manila, Philippines

Banuri, T and Holmberg J (1992) *Governance for Sustainable Development: A Southern Perspective.* IIED, Islamabad and London

Carley, M (1994) *Policy Management Systems and Methods of Analysis for Sustainable Agriculture and Rural Development.* IIED, London and FAO, Rome

Carley, M, and Christie, I (1992) *Managing Sustainable Development.* Earthscan, London

Commission on Resources and Environment (1993) *1992–93 Annual Report to the British Columbia Legislative Assembly.* Commission on Resources and Environment, Victoria (British Columbia)

Dalal-Clayton, DB and Dent D (1993) Surveys, Plans and People: A Review of Land Resource Information and its Use in Developing Countries. *Environmental Planning Issues* No 2, IIED, London

Falloux, F, and Talbot, L (1992) *Crisis and Opportunity: environment and development in Africa.* Earthscan, London

FAO (1991) *Strategy and Agenda for Action for Sustainable Agriculture and Rural Development.* FAO, Rome

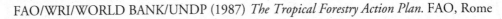

FAO/WRI/WORLD BANK/UNDP (1987) *The Tropical Forestry Action Plan.* FAO, Rome

Hill, J (1993) *National Sustainable Strategies. A Comparative Review of the Status of Five Countries: Canada, France, The Netherlands, Norway and UK.* Green Alliance, London

IMO (1983) *Strategy for the Protection of the Marine Environment.* International Maritime Organization, London

IUCN (November 1992) *Report of Workshops on Strategies for Sustainability in South and Southeast Asia and Africa.* IUCN, Gland, Switzerland

IUCN (July 1993) *Report of Workshop on Strategies for Sustainability in Latin America.* IUCN, Gland, Switzerland

IUCN (1994 a) *Strategies for Sustainability. Africa: Volume 1.* IUCN, Gland, Switzerland

IUCN (1994 b) *Strategies for Sustainability. Asia: Volume 1.* IUCN, Gland, Switzerland

IUCN (1994 c) *Strategies for Sustainability. Latin America: Volume 1.* IUCN, Gland, Switzerland

IUCN. 1984. *National Conservation Strategies: a Framework for Sustainable Development.* IUCN, Gland, Switzerland

IUCN/UNEP/WWF (1980) *World Conservation Strategy. Living resource conservation for sustainable development.* IUCN, UNEP and WWF, Gland, Switzerland

IUCN/UNEP/WWF (1991) *Caring for the Earth. A strategy for sustainable living.* IUCN, UNEP and WWF, Gland, Switzerland, and Earthscan, London

OECD (1987) Seminar on Strengthening Environmental Cooperation with Developing Countries (Report). OECD, Paris

OECD (1991) Recent Developments in the Use of Economic Instruments. *Environment Monographs* No 41. OECD, Paris

OECD (1992) Good Practices for Country Environmental Surveys and Strategies. *OECD Guidelines on Environment and Aid,* 2. OECD, Paris

Pretty, JN (1993) *Alternative Systems of Inquiry for a Sustainable Agriculture.* IIED, London

Rees, WT 1989. Defining sustainable development. *Research Bulletin,* UBC Centre for Human Settlements, Vancouver

SDC (1991) *Sustainability of Development Projects: Basic Principles and Application in Practice.* Swiss Directorate for Development Cooperation and Humanitarian Aid, Bern

Shah, P (1993) *Institutional Participation: Case study of Joint Forest Management Programme in India*. Paper presented to the Workshop on Strategies for Sustainability, IUCN General Assembly, 1994, Buenos Aires

UN (1948) *Universal Declaration of Human Rights*. UN Commission on Human Rights, Paris

UN (1982) *World Charter for Nature*. UN General Assembly 37th Session (UN/GA/RES/37/7), New York

UN (1992) *Rio Declaration on Environment and Development*. The UN Conference on Environment and Development, 3–14 June, Rio De Janiero

UNCED (1992) *Agenda 21*. United Nations General Assembly, New York

UNCHS (1976) *Vancouver Action Plan for Human Settlements*. Adopted by the UN Conference on Human Settlements (HABITAT), Vancouver

UNCOD (1977) *Plan of Action to Combat Desertification*. Adopted by the UN Conference on Desertification, Nairobi

UNDP/IADB (1990) *Our Own Agenda: Report of the Latin American & Caribbean Commission on Development and Environment*. Inter-American Development Bank, Washington DC, and United Nations Development Programme, New York.

UNEP/UNESCO (1975) *International Environmental Education Programme*. United Nations Environment Programme, Nairobi and United Nations Educational, Scientific and Cultural Organisation, Paris

UNWC (1977) *Mar del Plata Action Plan for Water Resources Development*. Adopted by the UN Water Conference, Mar del Plata, Argentina

WCED (1987) *Our Common Future*. Report of the World Commission on Environment and Development. Oxford University Press, Oxford

WHO (1981) *Global Strategy for Health for All by the Year 2000*. World Health Organization

WPC (1974) *World Population Plan of Action*. Adopted by the World Population Conference, Bucharest

WRI/IUCN/UNEP (1992) *Global Biodiversity Strategy: Guidelines for Action to Save, Study and Use Earth's Biotic Wealth Sustainably and Equitably*. WRI/IUCN/UNEP. World Resources Institute, Washington, DC

Strategies for National Sustainable Development

World Bank (1990) *National Environmental Action Plans in Africa.* Proceedings from a workshop organized by the Government of Ireland, the Environmental Institute, University College, Dublin, and the World Bank (EDIAR and AFTEN). World Bank, Washington, DC

World Bank (1991) *Issues Facing Environmental Action Plans in Africa.* Report from a Club of Dublin Workshop, Mauritius. World Bank, Washington, DC

World Bank (1992) Operational Directive 4.02: Environmental Action Plans. *The World Bank Operational Manual.* World Bank, Washington, DC

Glossary

ADB	Asian Development Bank
AKRSP	Aga Khan Rural Support Programme (Pakistan)
BCSD	Business Council for Sustainable Development
BRAC	Bangladesh Rural Advancement Centre
CBO	Community-based Organization
CEPA	Commonwealth Environment Protection Agency (Australia)
CI	Conservation International
CIDA	Canadian International Development Agency
CILSS	Permanent Committee for Drought Control in the Sahel
CSD	Commission on Sustainable Development
EAI	Enterprise for the Americas Initiative
ECODES	National Conservation Strategy for Sustainable Development (Costa Rica)
EIA	Environmental Impact Assessment
EPA	Environmental Protection Agency
EPC	Environmental Protection Council (Nepal)
ESD	Ecologically Sustainable Development (Australia)
FAO	Food and Agriculture Organization (UN)
GATT	General Agreement on Tariffs and Trade
GDP	Gross Domestic Product
GEF	Global Environment Facility
GINEF	Global Initiative on National Environment Funds
GNP	Gross National Product
GTZ	Deutsche Gesellschaft für Technische Zusammenarbeit
IADB	Inter-American Development Bank
IEC	Public Information, Education and Communications
IGAE	Inter-Governmental Agreement on the Environment (Australia)
IIED	International Institute for Environment and Development
IMF	International Monetary Fund
IMO	International Maritime Organization
IUCN	International Union for Conservation of Nature and Natural Resources (the World Conservation Union)
JRC	Journalists Resource Centre for the Environment (Pakistan)
LIRDP	Luangwa Integrated Resource Development Project (Zambia)

NCS	National Conservation Strategy	SIDA	Swedish International Development Authority
NEAP	National Environmental Action Plan	SPREP	South Pacific Regional Environment Programme
NEF	National Environment Funds	TFAP	Tropical Forestry Action Programme
NEMP	National Environment Management Plan	TNC	The Nature Conservancy
NEP	National Environment Programme	UN	United Nations
NEPAP	National Environment Policy and Action Plan (Nepal)	UNCED	United Nations Conference on Environment and Development (1992)
NEPP	National Environment Policy Plan (Netherlands)	UNCHS	United Nations Centre for Human Settlements
NESDS	National Ecologically Sustainable Development Strategies (Australia)	UNDP	United Nations Development Programme
NFAP	National Forestry Action Plan	UNEP	United Nations Environment Programme
NGO	Non-governmental Organization	UNESCO	United Nations Educational, Scientific and Cultural Organization
NORAD	Norwegian Agency for Development Cooperation	UNSO	United Nations Sudano-Sahelian Office
NPC	National Planning Commission (Nepal)	UPP	User Pays Principle
NSDS	National Sustainable Development Strategy	USAID	United States Agency for International Development
ODA	Overseas Development Administration (UK)	WB	World Bank
OECD	Organization for Economic Cooperation and Development	WCED	World Commission on Environment and Development
		WCS	World Conservation Strategy
ONE	Office National de l'Environnement	WHO	World Health Organization
PPP	Polluter Pays Principle	WMO	World Meteorological Organization
RAC	Resource Assessment Commission (Australia)	WRI	World Resources Institute
SDC	Swiss Development Corporation	WWF	World Wide Fund for Nature

Index